Virtual Activism on Cameroon: The Camnet Files

Isaac Njoh Endeley

Langaa Research & Publishing CIG
Mankon, Bamenda

Publisher
Langaa RPCIG
Langaa Research & Publishing Common Initiative Group
P.O. Box 902 Mankon
Bamenda
North West Region
Cameroon
Langaagrp@gmail.com
www.langaa-rpcig.net

Distributed in and outside N. America by African Books Collective
orders@africanbookscollective.com
www.africanbookcollective.com

ISBN: *9956-728-28-4*

DISCLAIMER
All views expressed in this publication are those of the author and do not necessarily reflect the views of Langaa RPCIG.

"One of the penalties for refusing to participate in politics is that you end up being governed by your inferiors."

Plato (428 BC - 348 BC)

"The worst illiterate is the political illiterate. He hears nothing, sees nothing, and takes no part in political life. He doesn't seem to know that the cost of living, the price of beans, of fish, of flour, of rent, of medicine, all depend on political decisions. He even prides himself on his political ignorance, sticks out his chest and says that he hates politics. He doesn't know, the imbecile, that from his political non-participation comes the prostitute, the abandoned child and, worst of all, corrupt officials, the lackeys of exploitative multinational corporations."

Bertrolt Brecht (1898 - 1956)

Table of Contents

iv

Preface

During the 1990s, as the Internet in general and e-mail in particular grew in popularity as a means of communication, a number of Cameroonians residing in various parts of the world established a vibrant and lively electronic forum for the discussion of various issues related to their native land. This Cameroonian Internet forum or network, known as Camnet, was hosted on computers based at the National Research Council (*Consiglio Nazionale delle Ricerche* - or CNR) in Italy. Camnet was literally an "open forum" both in the sense that any individual residing in any part of the world could subscribe or participate in the discussions and because the contributions were not monitored or censored.

Despite this lack of centralised control, Camnet was generally a highly disciplined forum and regular participants included some of Cameroon's foremost intellectuals who were already Internet-savvy by the 1990s. Camnet also attracted both supporters and opponents of the government in Yaoundé. Regardless of political party affiliations, ethnicity, religious views or other criteria, anyone interested in the affairs of Cameroon was welcome to participate. In fact, Camnet also benefited from periodic contributions from a number of foreigners interested in our country's affairs. Due to the quality of the debates that took place on the forum, it quickly became the leading medium for the dissemination of ideas and opinions on all things Cameroonian.

The Camnet forum demonstrated that Cameroonians living abroad (for whatever reason) could actively participate in the political, economic and social processes taking place in the country of their birth. Although in some cases they were thousands of miles away from Cameroon, they could contribute to the various dialogues and debates being conducted in their native land. This ability to remain actively engaged in the development of one's society and nation through the Internet is what is generally termed "virtual activism."[1] While in many cases activists have used the Internet to influence social issues and local politics, the focus of this book is on the ability of an electronic medium such as Camnet to fashion the dissemination of information and the formulation of opinions about Cameroon from great distances. It is my contention here that during its lifetime from the early 1990s until its demise in June 1999, the Camnet online forum distinguished itself as the first and most influential breeding ground for Cameroonian "virtual activism."

I feel very privileged to have been one of the regular contributors to the forum especially in the late 1990s and until the crash of the server at the CNR in mid-1999. Through these interactions with other "Camnetters," I learnt a great deal from many of my compatriots in various fields of endeavour. On many occasions I was impressed by the depth of thought and the quality of intellect exhibited by the contributors. In some instances I was challenged to rethink many preconceived notions. Those were exciting times and I will forever remain indebted to all the other contributors to the Camnet forum.

I should point out that although Camnet appeared to be dominated by political discussions, it was a truly multi-dimensional forum. No topic was explicitly forbidden and on some occasions the participants conducted extensive debates on issues that had nothing to do with Cameroon or with politics. In this publication, however, I have chosen to showcase mostly my own contributions with a direct bearing on Cameroon's development.

Moreover, although I was quite an active participant with very many contributions over the years, there was a tendency for the same

---

[1] There are, for instance, numerous web sites dealing specifically with the concept of "virtual activism" and attempting to characterize it. Among them, the following are worth mentioning: http://www.virtualactivism.org; http://webography.wordpress.com/2010/01/29/is-virtual-activism-not-real-activism/; and http://www.netaction.org/training/; http://www.sas.upenn.edu/sasalum/newsltr/winter07/virtual_activism.pdf (as of August 2012)

topics to resurface from time to time. Therefore, in order to avoid repetition, I have chosen in this compilation to present what may be considered as only a representative sample of my contributions.

To the extent possible, I have left the contributions intact. I have edited them only to correct glaring typographical errors but the substance, ideas and opinions remain unchanged. I have also maintained the dates and times of the initial e-mail as well as the subject lines of all the pieces in order to facilitate comparison and verification by other Camnetters who may wish to cross-check any aspects of the publication against their own records.

I have attempted in this work to limit myself mainly to my own writings and I quote others only to the extent necessary to place my comments in their proper context. In addition, whenever I have quoted other Camnet contributors, I have endeavoured to set their texts out in a different font size, often in italics and with a double indentation such that the contrast between theirs and mine is obvious. Due to the passage of time and the many changes that have taken place in people's individual circumstances, it has not been possible for me to contact the various Camnetters to notify them of my intension to quote from their writings. Efforts to solicit a reaction from some of the contributors quoted here have been fruitless, as my recent e-mail messages to their old addresses have bounced back. Nonetheless, in order to protect their privacy, I have excluded all of their e-mail addresses from this book.

The contributions contained in this compilation are primarily those I wrote from mid-1997 to mid-1999. This time frame is explained by two significant computer crashes I experienced. The first caused me to lose most of the contributions I had made prior to July 1997 and the second effectively ended my participation in Camnet. In fact, the June 1999 crash was so severe that it spawned the birth, at about the same time, of an alternative forum known as "Camnetwork" which exists to this day and is hosted on the Yahoo Groups servers.

Although the time frame of this publication is clearly defined, the contributions are not necessarily presented in chronological order.

Rather, I have chosen to adopt a thematic approach, creating several chapters and bringing together in each of them e-mail contributions and exchanges from different dates that deal with the same or related topics in a logical and coherent manner as reflected in the Table of Contents. It is my hope that the reader will find the subject lines of the individual e-mail messages sufficiently illustrative of the specific topic under discussion at any given point. In addition, whenever appropriate I have attempted to set the context for the reader by inserting a brief introductory passage at the start of each chapter, a little vignette setting the stage for each discussion.

A few of the contributions are in French and in order to reflect the bilingual nature of the debates that took place on Camnet, I have left them intact in the body of the text. However, for the benefit of readers who may not be very fluent in French, I have inserted the English translations in the form of footnotes.

It has taken me more than a decade to decide to publish this collection of my contributions to various debates that took place on Camnet in the 1990s. The individual articles are essentially short essays on my political philosophy. At the time when I wrote these essays I had no idea that they would one day be published to an audience beyond the immediate Camnet readership. This may be apparent from the tone and structure of the contributions, but this is also what makes this publication special. It is my hope that those who have had the opportunity to engage in debates in an online forum will appreciate the nature of the rapid-fire repartee that characterised the Camnet discussions. The context was quite different from today's web pages and blogs which afford their authors time and space to conduct extensive research in support of their opinions. The particularity of e-mail as a medium of communication is also that it personalises and humanises a discussion. In all of the contributions contained in this compilation, I feel as if I am talking directly to my friends and relatives. This remains true even in the instances where I disagree strongly with other contributors.

At a very personal level, I am struck by the currency of some of the issues with which I was preoccupied 15 years ago. For instance, the question of rampant corruption in Cameroon which was so widely discussed in 1997 is still very topical today; vote-rigging is still perceived to be a major problem at each election in Cameroon; President Biya's CPDM party is still firmly in control and exercises a virtual monopoly over the State apparatus despite the proliferation of political parties; the classic debate about "character" and "institutions" is still raging on; a number of the institutions provided for in the Constitution are yet to be established; the President continues to make frequent and lengthy trips to Europe for personal reasons; the criminal prosecution of perceived political opponents of the régime remains commonplace; and the question of the line of succession at the helm of the Cameroonian State is yet to be clarified.

I must say I am also not surprised that some of the predictions I made in the 1990s are a reality today. I predicted, for example, that if Cameroon's opposition political parties could not constitute a united front, Mr. Biya and his CPDM party might continue to preside over the fortunes of the country well into the 21st Century. Several presidential and parliamentary elections later, nothing has changed.

In the last two decades there has been a dramatic transformation in the nature of political participation not only in Cameroon and Africa but around the globe. Virtual activism is now commonplace; most governmental agencies and media organisations today have web pages where readers can glean the "official" version of any news story and leave comments if they like; almost everyone with a high school education and a mobile telephone can now have an e-mail address and a Facebook presence; individuals with the wherewithal can set up websites to promote a particular point of view; blogging has become commonplace and ordinary citizens are now able to express their views on a variety of subjects affecting their wellbeing. Whether the governments will take such input seriously is quite another matter.

These recent developments notwithstanding, it should always be borne in mind that in the Cameroonian context, the Camnet forum was a pioneer in the area of encouraging virtual activism. In an era when individual websites were still uncommon and information about Cameroon was centrally controlled by the government, Camnet, as a non-partisan forum, represented a welcome alternative.

I hope you will enjoy reading these contributions and, in the spirit of Camnet, I welcome any thoughts or opinions you may wish to share about this publication -- via e-mail, of course.

September 2012
Isaac Njoh Endeley
(Endeley@gmail.com)

Chapter I

On Cameroon Politics In General

Re: The 1997 Parliamentary Elections - Post Mortem

Introduction

Following the joint legislative and municipal elections of July 1997, the Camnet forum was the venue for a heated discussion regarding the outcome and implications of the vote. Most of the contributors agreed that the entire process was fatally flawed, but only a few made concrete proposals on the way forward. Professor John Mukum Mbaku of Utah State University in the USA was one of those whose contributions I found constructive in this regard. He posted well-written article in which he dissected the elections, analyzed the results and advanced a number of concrete proposals and hypotheses. My response below was in reaction to some of those hypotheses.

Date: Sun, 27 Jul 1997 23:03:17 -0400
Sender: CAMNET
From: Isaac Endeley
Subject:

Re: The 1997 Parliamentary Elections-Post Mortem

Dear John:

Like Taqyoba and Ebini before me, I'd like to thank you for initiating this discussion and for establishing a clear framework for analysis. Since I agree with the broad thrust of your argument, I will

1

endeavour to limit my comments only to selected segments of your text. Let me state, for the record, that I find your hypothesis (3) (b) to be by far the most plausible, even though it can hardly be distinguished from your interpretation (1). (To eliminate the ambiguity of having two scenarios labelled (3), I have created a (3) (a) and a (3) (b).)

You wrote:

The opposition, especially the SDF, threatened to boycott the national assembly, arguing that the election was 'stolen' by the SDF.

I suppose you mean here that the election was 'stolen' BY the CPDM or 'stolen' FROM the SDF?

(3)(b) The election was not competitive. Under existing institutional arrangements, the Cameroon people cannot determine their own government. The opposition lost again because the incumbent used national institutions to rig the elections in its favor.

No, the election was not competitive. With the incumbent CPDM-dominated government responsible for organising everything from voter registration to the counting of the ballots; with a party stalwart, Gilbert Andze Tsoungui, heading the Ministry of Territorial Administration that organised the vote; with the widespread intimidation of opposition sympathisers at registration time; with the incumbent president's hand-picked Supreme Court Judges responsible for declaring the results; with the Head of State modifying the boundaries of electoral constituencies by presidential decree on election day; with the government's spokesman, Communications Minister Augustin Kontchou Kouomegni, responsible for allocating air time on state-owned radio and television; with individual CPDM supporters such as village chiefs able to determine when polling begins or ends in their constituency; with a three-week time lag between the vote and the official

2

proclamation of the results; and in the absence of an independent electoral commission, how could the election possibly have been competitive?

The song has been sung long and loud that Cameroon's current institutional arrangements are deeply flawed. There is no clearer demonstration of this truism than the way President Biya and his clique appear to thwart the will of the Cameroonian people with impunity at every opportunity. The national interest is constantly being subverted, and the governmental apparatus manipulated, to suit the whims and caprices of a handful of unscrupulous elites.

But this is not about individuals; it is about institutions. What Cameroon needs is a set of viable institutions that can withstand the fluctuations of human character. The country needs institutions that inspire confidence and are not subject to the ebb and tide of political ambition or personal gain. These include (but are not limited to): a clear demarcation between political parties and the state; an independent and competent judiciary; a system of accountability for all legislators, government officials and other public servants; transparency in the conduct of public affairs; a system of governance involving the full participation of the governed at all levels; the full integration of all segments of the population, including all marginalised groups; an independent electoral commission; complete editorial freedom for the print and the broadcast media; etc.

QUESTION: Should self-determination for Southern Cameroon become a campaign issue in the presidential elections? Should each political party and its candidate be required to issue a white paper on this issue?

Yes indeed, to both questions. Any political party aspiring to form the national government or to have its candidate elected national president should be willing and able to address all questions of national importance. The Southern Cameroons issue (a.k.a. the Anglophone problem) is one of several critical problems facing the national government. Every party should be expected to devise its own formula for dealing with it.

3

Maybe the party and its leaders, do indeed, have a vision for the country. However, my problem is that I have not seen it.

Interesting point, John. I agree with you that all political parties and pressure groups should publicise and advertise more. But the simple fact that YOU are not familiar with a party's platform does not mean the party hasn't got one. I, for instance, am not an official of the SDF. Yet I am aware that the party has published a Draft Constitution of the Federal Republic of Cameroon and many other documents which are readily available on the Internet at:

http://www.winternet.com/~ndemeno/sdf.html

Even the Economist Intelligence Unit, in its Country Reports for the first two quarters of 1997, commended the SDF for coming up with an economic programme (NESPROG), a vision.

the SDF (and other opposition parties) should sit down and put such a vision on paper and have it published. In fact, I am willing to edit (only to meet publication standards--integrity of document will remain intact) such a white paper and publish it for mass circulation, either in one of the journals that I work with or as a book (I have secured a publisher in the UK).

This is a very generous offer and I hope some of the parties in Cameroon will be able to take advantage of it. The UNDP in particular --formerly the official parliamentary opposition party-- has done virtually nothing to reach out to Cameroonians in the diaspora and to the potential foreign investors you write about. That party would do well to heed your call.

Thanks again, John, for your comments and questions. I look forward to continuing the discussion.

Best regards,

Mola Njoh Endeley.

****

Re: Cameroon Politics

Introduction

In the aftermath of the October 1997 presidential elections in Cameroon, there was a lengthy debate on Camnet regarding what strategy the political opposition should adopt in light of the Biya régime's proven willingness and ability to manipulate the electoral process in its favour. In January 1998, a fellow Camnetter posted a series of news items describing the political tensions prevalent in Cameroon at the time. There is no need to reproduce all the news items here. My response below focused on just one news story that dealt with the possibility of the opposition SDF party entering into "negotiations" with the ruling CPDM party to form a coalition government.

On January 13, 1998, Julius Barthson wrote:

Hi Brothers and Sisters,
Here's some interesting news from home. Any comments?
Brother Julio.

Date: Sun, 18 Jan 1998 14:30:25 -0500
Sender: CAMNET
From: Isaac Endeley
Subject: **Re: Cameroon Politics**

Dear Brother Julio:

5

Thanks for sharing those news items. I do have a comment or two to spare with regard to this segment below.

Au sujet des négociations avec le RDPC (parti au pouvoir) --- Fru Ndi a précisé qu'il n'y a pas lieu de parler de négociations, mais plutôt de discussions. "We are not negotiating, we are just discussing " a martelé le leader anglophone. Dès le début de ces " discussions ", il avait nettement déclaré qu'il n'en attendait pas grand-chose, tablant sur ce qu'il a appelé " la mauvaise volonté du RDPC".[1]

First off, I must say I appreciate the distinction Mr. Fru Ndi makes between "discussions" and "negotiations" and I applaud the SDF's decision to pursue this strategy. There is no harm in maintaining a dialogue with one's opponents. In our Cameroonian context, such dialogue can only lead to a reduction in the political tensions and spates of violence that have cost us so much in the last eight years.

However, the SDF must not participate in any kind of "government of national unity" led by Mr. Biya's CPDM. By this I mean the SDF should not allow any of its members to be APPOINTED to any posts in Mr. Biya's ministerial cabinet. But it should maintain all the seats to which its members have been ELECTED, such as in the National Assembly and in various municipal councils. The SDF must continue to serve as the loyal opposition and to bide its time.

Cameroon is currently in danger of reverting to a one-party state and the SDF remains the last beacon of hope for all those who wish to see democracy flourish in the country. With the defection or cooptation of several former opposition stalwarts into the ranks of

---

[1] Translation: On the issue of negotiations with the ruling CPDM party, Mr. Fru Ndi stated that there were no negotiations but discussions. "We are not negotiating, we are discussing," the Anglophone leader emphasised. He had clearly stated from the beginning that he did not expect much from these "discussions" due to what he termed the "bad faith of the CPDM."

6

the ruling party, there is a certain apprehension that in the end there might not be any credible alternative to the Biya regime. Were the SDF to enter a CPDM government, such fears would become reality.

As we all know, one of the fundamental characteristics of a democracy is the existence of at least two separate political parties with a reasonable chance of capturing power. It is not enough merely for a multitude of parties to exist in a polity. What really matters is that there are at least two of them with decent prospects of forming a government.

A few well-known examples from around the world would serve to illustrate my point. In the U.S.A. the Republican and Democratic parties perform this function; in the U.K. it is the Conservative and Labour parties; in France the Gaullists (R.P.R.) and the Socialists alternate in power; and in Canada the Liberals and the Conservatives represent the two viable options. If Mexico, for instance, is not generally considered a democracy, it is not because that country lacks opposition parties. It is rather because, thus far, none of them has constituted a credible alternative to the appropriately named Institutional Revolutionary Party (P.R.I.) that has been in power forever.

In Cameroon so far the SDF has appeared as a credible alternative to the CPDM regime. It is important that this perception be maintained and that the freedom of the political market place be preserved. By "discussing" but "not negotiating" with the CPDM, the SDF is playing a crucial role in fostering democracy in the country. Admittedly, the playing field is far from being even, but Mr. Biya's intransigence cannot be everlasting. Sooner rather than later, one hopes, the conditions will be ripe for the demise of his dictatorship.

Peace,

Mola Njoh Endeley.

****

Re: CPDM-SDF Negotiations, The End?

Introduction

By February 1998, it had become apparent that the ruling CPDM party and the main opposition SDF party were not making any progress in their widely reported "discussions" and "negotiations." One Camnetter who found the situation particularly troubling posted an open letter to President Paul Biya on Camnet. I immediately seized the opportunity to place myself in the President's position and to give a likely response from his perspective. As indicated in the preface to the response, my reason for impersonating the President was purely for the purposes of debate and dialogue.

On February 13, 1998, Akere D.T wrote:

HIS EXCELLENCY: PAUL BIYA

MR. PRESIDENT- It is reported that your party, the Cameroon Peoples Democratic Movement (CPDM), has shown bad faith in the failed negotiations with the Social Democratic Front (SDF) intended to bring about peaceful political and constitutional change in Cameroon. It is also reported that you were in Europe on a vacation when these very important negotiations were going on, prompting many citizens including myself, to conclude that you placed little importance on their success.

As the leader of your party, and of the nation, I am therefore holding you mainly responsible for the failure of these negotiations. You and your supporters may not realize it, but Cameroon is on a very dangerous course. I am henceforth strongly requesting that you and your party respect the will of the majority of the Cameroonian people, as well as of the international community by re-opening serious discussions on the country's problems with all elements of the opposition. Don't you realize, Mr. President, that Cameroon\Cameroun as a Nation, is slowly but surely breaking up?

Date: Sat, 14 Feb 1998 00:03:21 -0500
Sender: CAMNET
From: Isaac Endeley
Subject: **Re: CPDM-SDF NEGOTIATIONS, THE END?**

Preface: Purely for the purposes of debate and dialogue, I will attempt here quite literally to play devil's advocate and to impersonate President Po Mbia.

Dear Mr. Akere D. Achu:

Thank you for your letter of February 13, 1998, in which you raised some very interesting issues. In my capacity as the Head of State and the leader of the CPDM, I will do my best to address each one of your concerns as honestly as possible.

Yes, it is true that ever since the October 12, 1997 presidential election, I have been trying to include as many opposition parties as possible in my government. I have so far managed to persuade some former opposition politicians, such as those from the UNDP and the UPC, to join my ministerial cabinet. Unfortunately, not everybody is willing to cooperate with me at this juncture. To that end, I have instructed certain members of my party, the Cameroon People's Democratic Movement (CPDM), to conduct negotiations with some other opposition parties, particularly the Social Democratic Front (SDF), with a view to resolving our differences. Contrary to your assertion, we are conducting these negotiations in good faith. We want peace and stability to continue to reign in our country.

However, at no point have I ever indicated to the SDF, or to anyone else for that matter, that I am willing to accede to some of their more extreme demands. All this talk about further constitutional change is just a waste of time. Didn't I just promulgate the amended constitution on January 18, 1996? So why do we need to amend it

9

again? A constitution is not like underwear, you know. You can't keep changing it every day! Besides, where was the SDF when the constitutional amendments were being discussed in the National Assembly in 1995? Whose fault is it that they had chosen to boycott the 1992 parliamentary elections?

It is true that I have been on vacation in Europe for the last several weeks, but that is hardly an indication of the level of importance I place on the negotiations. First of all, as a human being, a civil servant, and a Head of State, I am entitled to a vacation. Secondly, I personally ensured that my Prime Minister, Mr. Peter Musonge, would head the CPDM negotiating team. As you surely know, he is very widely respected for his competence and integrity. Thirdly, why is the SDF team being led by Mr. Nyo Wakai and not by Mr. Fru Ndi? My being abroad makes no difference, because even if I were home I would not be the one doing the negotiating.

Furthermore, you indicate your fear that Cameroon may have embarked on a dangerous course. Well, my dear compatriot, as your Head of State, I can assure you that Cameroon is doing just fine. Haven't you heard or read the latest reports from the international financial institutions? Our country is having all kinds of new loans from the World Bank and the IMF because of its high level of stability. As I stated during the last presidential campaign, I have ruled Cameroon for 15 years and I can rule it for 14 more years. I am in complete control and you need not worry. Should the present talks fail, we will revive them at a later date and carry on. This is not an emergency; the next scheduled elections (municipal) are almost three years away.

With regard to your request that my party and I "respect the will of the majority of the Cameroonian people", I must admit I am at a loss as to what you mean. Didn't my party win 117 out of 180 seats in parliament last May? Didn't I win the October 1997 presidential election with an unprecedented score of 92.5% of the vote? Isn't that sufficient evidence that the CPDM is the true choice of the Cameroonian people? The ones who need to show their respect for the will of the Cameroonian people are those who always boycott

10

elections. We in the CPDM are not afraid of any democratic challenge because we know we will always win.

Well, my dear countryman, I must stop here for now. Please feel free to contact me again with any further comments or questions. I look forward to pursuing the dialogue.

Your President,

Po Mbia.

(Impersonated by Isaac Njoh Endeley)

****

Re: SDF: Facts or fiction?

Introduction

As the reports about the "discussions" and "negotiations" between the ruling CPDM party and the opposition SDF party persisted through the first half of 1998, it became increasingly difficult to distinguish fact from fiction. For many casual observers, it remained unclear whether all the reports were merely a calculated attempt by the Biya régime to weaken the opposition in the eyes of the public or if the SDF was seriously considering forming an alliance with the CPDM "in the interest of national unity." The question posed by one Camnetter in July 1998 provided an opening to explore the role of some external factors in the Cameroonian political equation.

On July 19, 1998, Emmanuel J. Ndamukong pondered:

Dear camnetters,

It's hard to tell what is true these days in Cameroon politics. One cannot tell whether all these are exaggerated to weaken the SDF and coax them into a deal with the Biya government or depicts a reality. One can only hope that as bad as it is, Cameroon remains a multi-party state.

If the SDF must come out of the crisis head-high, all these issues raised either by dissidents or the press must be investigated thoroughly, openly, and democratically. Anything short of this may not settle the dust. Let's hope for the best. Peace.

Emmanuel Ndamukong

Date: Mon, 20 Jul 1998 00:11:35 -0400
Sender: CAMNET
From: Isaac Endeley
Subject: **Re: SDF: Facts or fiction?**

Hi, Emmanuel:

The question you raise in your caption above is the same one I've been asking myself for several months now. I imagine many other Camnetters are having similar misgivings. While it is difficult at this point to answer with absolute certainty, I believe it is fair to conclude that there is no smoke without fire. All the reports about the turmoil and turbulence brewing within the SDF certainly suggest that the party is facing serious teething problems.

One plausible explanation for the apparent change of heart among the SDF's Members of Parliament is that some of them are buying into the new logic of our Western partners. For instance,

12

whereas in the early 1990s the Americans encouraged the SDF to maintain a radical posture vis-à-vis the Biya regime, today the U.S. Embassy in Yaoundé is trying to mediate between the government and the opposition in order to ensure peace and stability for the construction of the Chad-Cameroon pipeline. As you know, American companies Exxon and Shell have a huge stake in the project. The Americans therefore have an interest in encouraging the SDF to join a "unity" government.

Furthermore, although the mission of the World Bank and IMF is officially restricted to the economic domain, these two institutions have been encouraging the Cameroonian government to resume and maintain a dialogue with the political opposition. The latest versions of the structural adjustment plans establish a clear relationship between political stability (but not necessarily democracy) and economic growth. It is widely believed within the Bretton Woods institutions that the recent economic gains can best be sustained and improved upon by getting all parties to work together.

In a nutshell, do not be puzzled if you learn one of these days that Mr. Biya and Mr. Ndi have agreed to work together "in the interest of national unity", or any such platitude.

Take care.

Mola Njoh Endeley.

****

Re: Voting Rights for Cameroonians in the Diaspora

Introduction:

In addition to disseminating information and sharing opinions about various issues affecting Cameroon, the members of the Camnet forum also undertook a number of concrete projects aimed

13

at directly impacting the lives of Cameroonians. These included: 1) a drive to rehabilitate a primary school in the District of Ngomo; 2) the creation of an investment club known as CamInvest; 3) an attempt to win the right to vote for Cameroonians residing outside the country; 4) the establishment of a Cameroon Renaissance Society (CRA) to coordinate the collection and dissemination of information about the country, among other things; 5) the creation of a Cameroon Scientific Society to promote the development of science in the country; and 5) follow-up regarding a petition we sent to the Head of State asking for accountability regarding the March 1997 armed attacks in the North-West Province that resulted in many deaths.

After several months of relative silence on these and other topics, one Camnetter asked for updates. In my capacity as one of those who volunteered to coordinate the effort regarding the third item on the list, I offered the update presented in the e-mail below in February 1998. The next e-mail, dated September 1998, is along the same thread.

On February 20, 1998, Kamguia Mu Fedjo wrote:

The following Camnet-born topics and projects would necessitate an update. Could the initiators and/or current heads oblige?

1- Ngomo School (Muke?)
2- Caminvest
3- Right to vote for the diaspora (Marius?)
4- CRA (Jerry?)
5- Cameroon Scientist (Bell?)
6- Petition to president for accountability in NW crackdown following attacks in March 1997 (KMF?)

[...]

By knowing what we have done with our projects so far, we may gain some insight into what we can realistically achieve in the future, and take corrective measures for the deficiencies, or revise our goals.

Date: Mon, 23 Feb 1998 01:01:27 -0500
Sender: CAMNET
From: Isaac Endeley
Subject: **Re: Request for updates**

Hello, KMF:

You have rendered the Camnet community a great service by resuscitating discussion on some projects initiated on this forum. Thank you for having the levelheadedness to raise these issues once again without undue antagonism. Such an approach as yours here can only lead to more fruitful dialogue.

With regard to item number 3 on your list above, I would like to reassure you and other Camnetters that the drive to obtain the right to vote for Cameroonians residing abroad is well under way. (Marius has been unable to participate fully in some of our most recent discussions, but I am in regular contact with him and I hope you don't mind if I respond in his stead.)

But first, it might be useful to briefly remind folks what this is all about. In October 1997, Marius Tegomoh advanced a proposal aimed at obtaining the right to vote for all Cameroonians living abroad. The proposal was thoroughly debated on this forum, and December 31st, 1999 was set as the deadline by which we would like to accomplish the task. It was further established that this would necessitate a constitutional amendment and a modification of the prevailing electoral laws in order to insert a clause that explicitly recognises our right to vote. Because it is non-partisan and will benefit each one of us equally, the proposal appears to enjoy wide support. Pursuant to our discussions, it was agreed that the first step would be to constitute a comprehensive data base of Cameroonians in the diaspora.

Unfortunately, only a handful of people have volunteered to help coordinate the drive in their respective areas of residence: Marius Tegomoh and Levai Babaya (Minnesota); Steve Andoseh (Washington Metropolitan Area); Isaac Zama (Wisconsin); and Isaac Endeley (Canada). Nevertheless, we have been working behind the scenes to keep the momentum going and we strive to maintain regular communication among the coordinators. A few weeks ago I sent Marius the list of all the names and addresses I had compiled so far, and we know that Steve and Isaac are also rounding up their lists at this very moment.

Meanwhile, it needs to be pointed out that it is not too late for other Camnetters to volunteer to lead the drive in their respective communities. It would be greatly appreciated if a couple of compatriots in the UK, France, Germany and other European countries could agree to give us a hand here. Netters in other U.S. communities not yet covered are also invited to provide assistance. Alternatively, individual Cameroonians who wish to have their names and addresses added to the data base can transmit the relevant information to any of the following:

Ndemeno Tegomoh
Levai Babaya
Steve Andoseh
Isaac Zama
Isaac Endeley

The next few steps will involve examining Cameroon's current electoral laws, working out the wording of the draft amendment(s), and devising a strategy for implementation, among other things. JMP Yabiango gracefully set the ball rolling by forwarding us a New York Times story last November about how the Dominican diaspora managed to achieve objectives similar to ours. We also had the occasion to contemplate excerpts of the Canada's Constitution and

16

electoral laws with provisions for citizens residing abroad. Anyone with further information on similar issues should feel free to share it with the rest of us. Particularly welcome will be copies of Cameroon's electoral laws.

As you can see, KMF, this project is very much alive and there is still a lot of room for others to provide their own input. With the imminent completion of the preliminary stage, it is hoped that many more people will be able contribute to its ultimate success. As stated earlier, it is a non-partisan proposal that will benefit each one of us equally, regardless of our affiliations. I'm sure we're justified in our optimism.

Warmest regards,

Mola Njoh Endeley.

****

Re: Voting Rights for Cameroonians in the Diaspora

Introduction:

It was announced on Camnet that Cameroon's Minister of External Relations would be visiting New York in September 1998 to attend a session of the United Nations General Assembly and would probably be having a general meeting with all interested Cameroonians in the New York area. Taking advantage of the opportunity, I prepared a submission to the Honourable Minister on the subject of the right of Cameroonians in the Diaspora to cast a vote in elections. I did not receive any acknowledgement of receipt from the purported conduit and I do not know if the memorandum was ever delivered to the Minister. Nonetheless, it is important to demonstrate that the struggle for Cameroonians abroad to participate in the electoral process started a long time ago and it is indeed gratifying to note that it has now been recognised.

On September 25, 1998, "Johnspvm1@..." wrote:

On behalf of the President of Camsa, Tata Ngonga Alex, I wish to inform all Cameroonians (students & non-students) that the Minister of External Relations, H.E. Augustin Kontchou Kouomegni will be in the US next week.

A meeting has been scheduled for us to meet with the Minister on Tuesday, October 6, 1998 at the Cameroonian Mission in New York.

Reservations could be made by fax to 973 674 3108 or to this e-mail address. Please kindly pass the information to other brothers and sisters.

A second circular will be sent Monday 28th September, 1998 with exact time of the meeting with directions to the Mission.

Further questions, do not hesitate to contact us.

Fraternally yours,

M. Disame
Special Advisor

Date: Sun, 4 Oct 1998 12:06:10 -0400
Sender: CAMNET
From: Isaac Endeley
Subject: Re: (Invitation - Kontchou in New York)

Dear M. Disame:

I am sorry I cannot attend the meeting with the Honourable Minister of State for External Relations, scheduled to take place in New York on Tuesday, October 6, 1998. I would be grateful if you could kindly forward this memorandum to him.

Thanks in advance.

I.N. Endeley.

To: His Excellency Pr. Augustin Kontchou Kouomegni
Minister of State in charge of External Relations

Subject: The Right to Vote

Your Excellency:

I have the honour of writing to you to solicit your counsel and support for a legislative project. Over the last several months, some of us, Cameroonians currently residing away from home, have been exploring the possibility of winning the right to participate in the political process in Cameroon. We are particularly interested in obtaining for ourselves and other members of our diverse communities in the 'diaspora' the right to vote in Cameroon's national elections. What we have in mind is to enact a revision of the current electoral laws that would benefit each and every member of

19

the Cameroonian Community abroad equally, regardless of their political affiliation or ethnic origin. This is a non-partisan initiative.

I am writing to you because, the way I view it, if such a scenario were to come to pass, the voting would be conducted through the Cameroonian embassies abroad. In your capacity as the Minister of State in charge of External Relations, you are directly responsible for the conduct of affairs at those embassies.

To that end, Your Excellency, I would like to address the following questions to you:

1) Do you consider such a move desirable?

2) Do you find the proposal feasible?

3) What, in your informed opinion, do we need to do to bring this project to fruition?

Your Excellency, just in case you are wondering why those of us currently residing away from home would want to participate in the political process in Cameroon, here are a few reasons:

1) Wherever we may be right now, we are, first and foremost, citizens of Cameroon and we remain attached to our roots.

2) Many of us contribute financially to our country's economic development (e.g. by investing in businesses or community projects) and to its human-resource development (e.g. by sponsoring relatives at schools and universities or by sending donations to our 'alma mater'). We would like to have a say, direct or indirect, in the decision-making process.

3) Some of us plan to return home for good at the earliest reasonable opportunity, and we would like some reassurance before embarking on such a trip.

Thank you, Honourable Minister, for your kind attention. I look forward to reading from you at your earliest convenience.

Sincerely.

Isaac Njoh Endeley.

****

Re: Acknowledgement of Receipt

Introduction

Following a series of armed attacks against government facilities in the North-West Province in March 1997, the Biya régime was reported to have embarked on a brutal crackdown of its real or perceived opponents in the area. Camnetters were deeply troubled by the accounts of repression, illegal arrests and extended periods of detention without charge or trial. In May 1997, we resolved to write a letter to President Paul Biya expressing our concerns. That historic letter, drafted in English and French, was electronically "signed" by about 150 Cameroonians residing in different parts of the world but brought together under the Camnet umbrella.

Mindful of the Cameroon government's reputation for ignoring negative criticism and for not engaging in a dialogue with anyone perceived as an adversary, the Camnet community was delighted that the Yaoundé régime acknowledged receipt of the petition -- five months after it was sent! My e-mail here was intended as a commendation for all those involved in the petition drive and as an encouragement to undertake such civic action in future. (See the footnote for an English translation of the e-mail.)

Date: Thu, 9 Oct 1997 00:33:59 -0400
Sender: CAMNET
From: Isaac Endeley
Subject: **Re: Accusé de réception**

Chers amis:

J'aimerais joindre ma voix à celles des frères Jean Modeste Dogmo et Pierre Faa pour féliciter Kamguia Mu Fedjo et tous les autres signataires de la pétition adressée à l'endroit du Président de la République en mai dernier. La façon dont l'action a été menée ici sur Camnet, ainsi que la réponse qu'elle a obtenue jusqu'ici, me font croire que tout n'est pas perdu pour notre chère patrie. Je tiens en particulier a remercier KMF d'avoir pris l'initiative et d'avoir fait preuve d'une astuce extraordinaire dans la coordination du projet. Il est à souhaiter que cette véritable 'leçon de culture démocratique' nous servira de base de comparaison dans toutes nos démarches futures. Il se peut bien que cet accusé de réception soit le dernier mot que l'on entendra du Palais de l'Unité, mais au mois nous pourrons toujours être fiers d'avoir agi quand l'action s'est avérée nécessaire.

Bravo à tous les pétitionnaires !²

---

² Dear Friends:

I would like to join my brothers Jean-Modeste Dogmo and Pierre Faa in congratulating Kamguia Mu Fedjo and all the other signatories of the petition we sent to the President of the Republic last May. The manner in which the effort was coordinated here on Camnet, as well as the response we have so far received, lead me to believe that all is not lost for our beloved fatherland. I would like in particular to commend KMF for taking a lead role and for showing extraordinary skill in coordinating the drive. It is to be hoped that this real "lesson in democratic culture" will serve as a standard against which our future endeavours will be measured. Even if this acknowledgement of receipt is the last communication we receive from Unity Palace, we can forever be proud of having acted when action was necessary.

22

Mola Njoh Endeley.

****

Re: Cameroon Politics - Um Nyobe and the UPC

Introduction

In August 1998 a fellow Camnetter posted an analysis of one of Cameroon's oldest political parties, the *Union des populations du Cameroun* (UPC) and its deceased leader Ruben Um Nyobe. I found the analysis truly enlightening and delightful in several respects. Since I generally agreed with the author's conclusions, I used only his concluding paragraph as a launching pad for the expression of my own thoughts and ideas about the spectacular failure of the UPC in the Cameroonian political arena.

Date:	Sun, 16 Aug 1998 19:29:53 -0400
Sender:	CAMNET
From:	Isaac Endeley
Subject:	**Re: Cameroon Politics - Um Nyobe and the UPC**

Hello, Steve:

I found your "panoramic profile" of the UPC very enlightening indeed. Your account of the movement's rise and demise certainly underscores the complexity of the Cameroonian polity, and one lesson I derived from it is that ideology should always be tempered with pragmatism. In my opinion, the UPC and its leaders might have fared a little better had they borne this in mind. It is a pity that some of our country's contemporary politicians appear to be repeating

---

those same mistakes. Since I agree with the broad thrust of your analysis, I will limit my comment to this excerpt from your concluding paragraph.

The combination of French atrocities, the early deaths of its principal founders, the incipient ethnicity of political action in Cameroon, and the insidious manipulations of Ahmadou Ahidjo, account for the paradox in the legacy of the UPC; that is, that a party could so successfully capture the aspirations of its people and still fail to garner its support.

Actually, I don't think it's much of a paradox that the UPC's perceived or purported popularity failed to transform itself into tangible gestures of support from the larger population. This seems to have been a classic case of the battle for people's hearts and heads (quite akin to the scenario being played out in the country today). If the party's aspirations coincided with people's in the 1940s and 1950s, it was mostly to the extent that everyone wanted independence. Where they parted company was on the shape that the independent state would assume. Like most movements cast in the Marxist-Leninist mould, the UPC tended to be rigid and monolithic. As a result, it was unable to placate fears emanating from two fronts.

On the one hand, the French colonialists were apprehensive of what might become of their interests in the territory after independence. (Sekou Touré's alliance with the Soviet Bloc in 1958 was not an experience the French were willing to see repeated in Cameroon.) Unfortunately, the UPC leaders were not sufficiently pragmatic to assuage any such misgivings, hence their persecution. It was a monumental error to mount a military campaign against an enemy that was significantly better equipped and more organised. The party also appears to have underestimated France's ability to use violence and intimidation as political weapons. With the Ahidjo regime as a convenient proxy, the French succeeded in portraying UPC militants as terrorists (*'maquisards'*), thus justifying their use of wanton brutality to repress the movement.

On the other hand, the party was unable to reassure the locals of their future under a UPC government. In fact, as you point out in your analysis, even in the *relatively free* elections to the pre-independence Consultative Assembly, the party never managed to win many seats. I don't think ethnicity was a major factor at that point, since the UPC hierarchy was composed of intellectuals from different parts of the country and the party had pockets of support across the territory (Bassaland, Bakossiland, Bamilekeland, Betiland, Douala, Southern Cameroons, etc). The main irony here is perhaps the fact that the party undertook most of its activities in areas where the free-enterprise ethos was already becoming firmly implanted. The traditional constituency of Marxist-Leninist movements --the proletariat, labour unions, and the disenfranchised urban masses-- made up only a small proportion of Cameroon's population in those days. As one might imagine, convincing budding capitalists and a burgeoning bourgeoisie to abandon their dreams in the pursuit of ideology (and a communist ideology at that!) was an up-hill task which the UPC never fully accomplished.

In the end, the party's lack of flexibility, or its unwillingness to compromise, might best account for its spectacular lack of success. Ideological extremism was never the forte of the Cameroonian populace, preoccupied as it has always been with its physical and material well-being. The recent splintering of the UPC into several "tendencies" is probably an indication that some of its leaders (A. F. Kodock, H. H. Nlend) may have learnt their lesson from the past and may have become more pragmatic, while others (N. Ntumazah) may still be hard-core ideologues. Furthermore, although much has been said and written about the persecution of the UPC leadership by the French and Cameroonian governments, relatively little has been revealed about the atrocities perpetrated by the ideological fanatics of that party on an unwitting population. This aspect of our country's history continues to fascinate me and I hope to keep learning about it.

Peace.

****

Re: Indonesia Regains its Freedom - temporarily!

Introduction

In May 1998, Indonesia's long-time dictator General Suharto was forced to resign following a widespread and violent protest across his country. In consequence, Camnetters had the occasion to conduct a discussion regarding the possibility of a peaceful succession at the helm in Cameroon. Of particular interest to me was the question as to whether it was legal for President Suharto to be replaced by his hand-picked successor, Vice-President B. J. Habibie. In that regard I had the opportunity in the e-mail below to explore the historical context and to examine the applicable provisions of the Cameroon Constitution.

Date: Thu, 21 May 1998 23:17:03 -0400
Sender: CAMNET
From: Isaac Endeley
Subject: **Re: Indonesia Regains its Freedom - temporarily!**

On May 21, 1998, Cecile Siewe wrote:

Suharto's current term was supposed to expire in a few months, at which time there would have been elections. Now not only has he handpicked his successor, he has decreed that the successor must rule for at least five years, until the year of our lord 2003!

Hello, Cecile:

Just a quick point here. Suharto was "re-elected" (unopposed) to a seventh consecutive five-year term on March 10, 1998. That term expires in March 2003 and it is the one Habibie is being called upon to complete. This is standard political practice the world over. In Cameroon, for example, when President Ahmadou Ahidjo, who had been "re-elected" to another five-year term in 1980, decided to step down in November 1982, his hand-picked successor Paul Biya was invited to complete the term of office. In the U.S., the term of the assassinated President Kennedy was completed by Vice-President Johnson while that of the disgraced Nixon was assumed by V-P. Ford. Meanwhile, I agree with you that it is probably too soon to pop the champagne in Habibie's honour.

Imagine then that Biya finally concedes, but demands that "Zero Mort" must be his replacement, and must rule for another 7 years - with the full backing of the army.

<chuckle> This is not an implausible scenario -- *"impossible n'est pas camerounais"*, as they say on the other side of the Mungo River. If I'm not getting my wires crossed here, Mr. "Zero Mort" is the gentleman who claims that a good player will always have a team. (He probably fancies himself as the Roger Milla of Cameroonian politics.) A couple of years ago, during the last municipal elections, I noticed that in Yaoundé at least, his close ties to the ruling team had earned him the street name "Atangana Kontchou". It would be really interesting to see who the fans of his new team would be if your scenario were to come to pass.

But beyond speculation, here is what Mr. Biya's January 18, 1996 Constitution stipulates with regard to succession at the helm:

****

Constitution of Cameroon

PART II: Executive Power

CHAPTER I: The President of the Republic

Article 6

Paragraph 4
"Where the office of President of the Republic becomes vacant as a result of death, resignation or permanent incapacity duly ascertained by the Constitutional Council, the polls for the election of the new President of the Republic must be held not less than 20 (twenty) days and not more than 40 (forty) days after the office becomes vacant.

(a) The President of the Senate shall as of right act as interim President of the Republic until the new President of the Republic is elected. Where the President of the Senate is unable to exercise these powers, they shall be exercised by his Vice, following the order of precedence.

(b) The interim President of the Republic --the President of the Senate or his Vice-- may neither amend the Constitution nor the composition of the Government. He may not organize a referendum or run for the office of President of the Republic.

Paragraph 5
Candidates for the office of President of the Republic must be Cameroonian by birth, enjoy their civic and political rights and must have attained the age of 35 (thirty-five) by the date of the election.

Paragraph 6
The conditions for electing the President of the Republic shall be laid down by law."

****

Needless to point out that with the Constitutional Council and the Senate yet to be created, Cameroon could easily slide into chaos if Biya were to fall into any one of the many traps awaiting him at every turn. As "Zero Mort" put it a while ago, there are vultures among us waiting to devour any carcasses. In the absence of an obvious successor, we might not be as lucky as the Indonesians. Some may derive their inspiration from such uncertainty; others may find it appalling. It all depends on one's perspective.

Best regards,

Mola Njoh Endeley.

****

Date: Thu, 21 May 1998 23:16:53 -0400
Sender: CAMNET
From: Isaac Endeley
Subject: **Re: Indonesia Regains its Freedom - temporarily!**

On May 20, 1998, Levai Babaya wrote:

Leadership is like gambling; you should know when to call the other person's bluff.

Dear Brother Levai:

I like this simile you've used here because it really captures the essence of Cameroon: a political casino. Has it occurred to you that the main reason why our "leader" Paul Biya has managed to stay in power this long is that he has always known exactly when to call the opposition's bluff? Consider the following, if you will:

29

* During the "ghost-town" operation, when the opposition parties attempted to bring life across the country to a standstill, Mr. Biya called their bluff and things soon returned to normal, at no cost to the ruling clique.

* When the opposition parties threatened to boycott all future elections unless an independent electoral commission was created, Mr. Biya called their bluff and all subsequent elections have been hotly contested [despite the continued absence of an independent electoral commission].

* When the same opposition parties warned that violence would erupt unless there was some power-sharing arrangement between themselves and the ruling CPDM, Mr. Biya called their bluff and he remains in complete control of all aspects of life in the country.

* When certain opposition figures were going around the world asking the international community to impose sanctions on Cameroon, Mr. Biya called their bluff and has since received greater amounts of foreign capital (e.g. Chad-Cameroon pipeline, ESAF from the Bretton Woods duo, new loans from France, Canada, Italy, China, Germany, etc).

* When the major opposition leaders pledged not to join the incumbent government, Mr. Biya called their bluff and some of them were enticed with plum posts.

Bottom line: most of our opposition figures lack solid principles and genuine commitment, making it a very easy gamble for Mr. Biya. At this rate he will continue to call their bluff and it is not inconceivable that he might last longer in power than Suharto did.

I still believe that people generally deserve the type of government they have. If we didn't deserve Paul Biya he wouldn't be there today. We would have kicked him out long ago!

Peace,
Mola Njoh Endeley.

****

Re: Constitutional Experts: Paul Biya 2004

Introduction

In early 1999, the Economist Intelligence Unit (EIU) published a country report on Cameroon in which it seemed to suggest that President Biya was constitutionally barred from seeking reelection at the end of his term in October 1997. As might have been expected, this suggestion prompted an impassioned discussion on Camnet. On the one hand, some agreed with the suggestion that President Biya could not legitimately seek another term in office. On the other hand, a few Camnetters thought the EIU's interpretation of the situation was inaccurate. In response to a specific question from one Camnetter, I examined the relevant provisions of the Cameroon Constitution and ventured an answer. Obviously, my interpretation has been borne out by the passage of time and the unfolding of events.

On March 22, 1999, Pa Fru Ndeh wrote:

According to this report, the January 1996 Constitution stipulates that Paul Biya is to step down in 2004 if he adheres to this Constitution. Could those who are very knowledgeable on constitutional affairs please clarify my understanding in this regard.

I am made to understand that the constitution cannot be applied retroactively. What does this mean if it holds true?

[...]

31

CONSTITUTION OF THE REPUBLIC OF CAMEROON

Law No. 96-06 of 18 January 1996 to amend the Constitution of 2 June 1972

[...]

PART II: EXECUTIVE POWER

CHAPTER I: THE PRESIDENT OF THE REPUBLIC

[...]

Article 6
1) The President of the Republic shall be elected by a majority of the votes cast through direct, equal and secret universal suffrage.

2) The President of the Republic shall be elected for a term of office of 7 (seven) years. He shall be eligible for re-election once.

[...]

Date: Wed, 24 Mar 1999 02:00:47 -0500
Sender: CAMNET
From: Isaac Endeley
Subject: **Re: Constitutional Experts: Paul Biya 2004**

Dear Pa Fru:

Whereas I do not consider myself a "constitutional expert", my interpretation of the above excerpt is that President Biya is entitled to stand for re-election in 2004. (This, unfortunately, might mean the EIU's understanding is erroneous.) The law was promulgated in January 1996 and is forward-looking rather than "retroactive". Were it the latter, Mr. Biya's previous terms of office would have rendered him ineligible for re-election in October 1997, having been previously "elected" in 1984, 1988 and 1992. It is therefore not inconceivable that he could stay in power until October in The Year Of Our Lord 2011.

"Blessed Be Cameroon" indeed!

Mola Njoh Endeley.

****

Biya in Europe ... Again!

Introduction

The issue of President Biya's frequent and extended trips to Europe has long been a subject of discussion on Cameroonian media outlets and Camnet was no exception. My e-mail here was triggered by a July 1998 news report from the Isaha'a Boh news agency, which stated that the President had once again taken off on another "brief stay in Europe," barely a month after returning from the previous one. In fact, this was the President's fourth trip to Europe in six months.

Cameroon-politics: President Paul Biya leaves Yaoundé for Europe

YAOUNDE, July 26 (Isaha'a Boh) - Cameroon's president Paul Biya, left the capital Yaoundé early Sunday for Europe, state radio has announced reading from a statement from the Civil Cabinet of the Presidency.

According to the statement, Mr. Biya has gone on a "brief stay in Europe". No details have been given.

The last time Mr. Biya was in Europe was last June when he attended the World Cup opening game and then went on to attend Cameroon's France 98 opening match against Austria.

Date:	Wed, 29 Jul 1998 12:27:59 -0400
Sender:	CAMNET
From:	Isaac Endeley
Subject:	**Biya in Europe ... Again!**

* In February 1998 (during the Nsam fire disaster) this guy was in Geneva, Switzerland on a "private visit".

** In May 1998 he was in Paris, France on a "private working visit" and to chat with his boss Jacques Chirac.

*** In June 1998 he was again in France to attend the World Cup football championship and to bring our Indomitable Lions good luck. Ha!

**** In July 1998 he is once more on a "brief stay in Europe".

At least FOUR trips to Europe in SIX months. What a job! What a life!

Vive le Cameroun ! Vive Po Mbia !

Mola Njoh Endeley.

34

****

Biya in Europe ... Again!

Introduction

In August 1998, a Camnetter residing in Geneva, Switzerland "mistakenly" posted on Camnet a private message apparently intended for a different audience. In the thinly coded private message, the author seemed to be saying that a person under observation was seriously "sick" and was staying at a Geneva hotel that was now surrounded by "tons of bodyguards" and had "many black men ... just standing under the tree." However, the cat was already out of the bag and it immediately became apparent to the Camnet audience that President Biya was, in fact, the subject under observation and that he staying at the Intercontinental Hotel in Geneva. Furthermore, despite the writer's subsequent request for his fellow Camnetters to disregard the contents of the first message, the speculation surrounding President Biya's health and the reason for his extended stay in Europe could not be overlooked.

First message from "Packaging Intern2@..." :

I am glad to hear from you again. Unfortunately I am not able to tell how serious is this guy sick. I have tried to get to know who is his doctor here so I can get close even by 'tricking' one of his/her assistants, but it is difficult. Where the guy stays is one block from my hostel, but guess what, there are tons of body guards in civilian dresses around here. If you are familiar with the place you will know the man is here. All of a sudden, there many black men in the hotel neighborhood, just standing under the tree. A very good friend of mine will be visiting this week end for "Les Fetes de Genève" and called me yesterday to request a good hotel to stay at and you guess my answer was Intercontinental... If he goes there then I will get the chance to get close without having people ask me where and why I am coming...

35

Have a good week end and I will tell more when I have the chance.

Thierry

Second message *from "Packaging Intern2@...."*

On August 7, 1998, Packaging Intern2 (Thierry??) wrote:

Dear all,
I am sorry to have polluted your mailboxes with a message which has nothing to do with this list. Disregard it.
Thanks

Thy

Date:	Sat, 8 Aug 1998 16:54:14 -0400
Sender:	CAMNET
From:	Isaac Endeley
Subject:	Re: Disregard a previous message

Hello, Thy:

There's no need to apologise. Your coded message below was very informative. We all know WHO "this guy" is, and thanks to that posting, we now also know exactly WHERE he is hiding and WHY. Anyone who saw those pathetic TV shots of the VIP tribune during the Cameroon-Austria match at France '98 would understand. It was quite obvious that someone was trying against all odds to prove Pius Njawé wrong. I hope your friend succeeds in getting a room at the Intercontinental Hotel. That way, perhaps you can "trick" the doctor's assistant or "get close" without being bothered by the "many black men in the hotel neighborhood". Please keep us posted.

36

(Btw, the "very good friend" you're expecting is not by any chance our Captain Guérandi, is it? Oh, well. Never mind. Just a thought...)

Take care.

Mola Njoh Endeley.

****

Re: Did the government criminalize the law suit against Fru Ndi et al?

Introduction

In February and March of 1999, Mr. John Fru Ndi, the leader of the main opposition SDF party, was involved in a law suit that many observers believed was politically motivated. This perception was also fuelled, at least in part, by the fact that the "discussions" and "negotiations" between the ruling CPDM party and the SDF had now broken down irretrievably. In the e-mail below, I attempted to point out that this was not the first time the Biya régime was trying to settle political scores through the law courts. The political dispute between President Biya and his predecessor, Ahmadou Ahidjo, had also followed that route. In fact, some thirteen years later, the régime is still very much in the business of prosecuting –and even persecuting– its real or perceived political opponents. In particular, many of the most serious contenders for the presidency have been incarcerated.

Date: Fri, 5 Mar 1999 03:11:01 -0500
Sender: CAMNET
From: Isaac Endeley
Subject: **Re: Did the government criminalize the law suit against Fru Ndi et al?**

Hello, My Amigos and Amigas:

Here's my own two cents' worth of legal mumbo jumbo. I believe the practice of criminalising civil suits in Cameroon predates the December 1990 law. Long before the *Kamdoum vs. Fru Ndi* case, two other prominent political figures had duked it out in a Yaoundé courthouse ... Well, sort of. The accused was actually tried *in absentia* by a military tribunal.

The date was 1984. The plaintiff, my main man Po Mbia. The defendant, his predecessor Baba Ahidjo. The charge, "*outrage contre le Chef de l'État*". And the verdict? Now, that's what's interesting here.

In addition to being sentenced to death for fomenting a *coup d'état*, former President Ahidjo was fined the sum of 20 million CFA francs for describing our new Head of State as "*faible et fourbe*" (among other horrible, horrible things). In other words, the ex-dictator was supposed to pay us 20 million for the insult, and then we would shoot him! (Let the record reflect the fact that the death sentence was later commuted to life imprisonment, but the former tyrant elected to wither away in exile --without paying us even a single franc!)

What's the point of all this? Nice of you to ask. Those in search of a precedent will recognise it right away. A leopard does not change its spots into stripes simply because a new piece of writing is rubber-stamped into law by an undemocratic parliament. Law or no law, the Cameroonian government does whatever it wants with any kind of case. Distinctions between the different types of law suits (civil, criminal, etc.) are for mere mortals. "*Le Cameroun, c'est le Cameroun.*"

Enuff said.

I'm outta here.
Mola Njoh Endeley.

****

Re: Banana Diplomacy: How does Cameroon fit in?

Introduction

As I assert in the preface, many foreigners interested in the affairs of Cameroon also participated regularly and freely in the Camnet discussions. Some of them shared their views and opinions as well as information or research findings with other Camnetters and solicited our reactions on a wide variety of issues affecting Cameroon. In this instance my reaction was triggered by what I considered to be the patronising attitude of a foreigner who was urging Cameroonians not to spend too much energy on issues like corruption, democracy and human rights, but to focus instead on investing in tangible goods for our families. I should point out that I still have not met the individual with whom I had this exchange and I do not know his nationality, or indeed whether he is a real person or a genuine foreigner. However, as with all of my other contributions to Camnet, what mattered was the message rather than the messenger.

Date: Mon, 15 Mar 1999 00:02:22 -0500
Sender: CAMNET
From: Isaac Endeley
Subject: **Re: Banana Diplomacy: How does Cameroon fit in?**

Dear Mike Lamson:

Over the years I've enjoyed reading your contributions from the ground in Yaoundé, but I'm afraid your latest posting is not among my favourites. I take strong exception to what I consider a patronising attitude exhibited in your piece excerpted below. (I guess I should also apologise in advance if my comments hereafter sound rather harsh.) As an expatriate (perhaps a white man), you automatically qualify for special treatment in your interactions with the Cameroonian authorities. You are, therefore, unable to appreciate the level of frustration that Cameroonian citizens feel when dealing with their own government.

You wrote:

Sometimes we spend so much energy on corruption, democracy, human rights and other issues that are quite grand but really not practical at this time.

In whose opinion are these issues "not practical at this time"? What gives you the authority to determine what is "practical" for us? You may not consider corruption a problem in Cameroon because, as an expatriate, you have easy access to all the amenities you require. Talk to some Cameroonians, including some Camnetters, who refused to pay a bribe and had to wait in vain for over two years to have electricity or a telephone line. Then you may begin to understand. You may think human rights issues are "not practical at this time", but I bet you those Cameroonians whose relatives have been brutalised by the so-called forces of law and order think otherwise. Did your own native country become developed by neglecting to address the issues of corruption, democracy and human rights?

All these issues will become a reality in Cameroon with time and the international community is pushing these issues.

Do you know how long we have been waiting for these issues to "become a reality in Cameroon"? From the days of slavery, through the age of colonialism, to this era of neo-colonialism, we have been patient. How much longer do you suggest we wait? That philosophy of being passive witnesses to our own history is what put us in this mess in the first place! We waited and waited patiently while our national wealth was plundered with impunity by both internal and external agents. When finally we start taking control of our own destiny, we are being told to relax because "all these issues will become a reality in Cameroon with time". You can take such advice somewhere else. There's no turning back for us!

I suggest that everyone work in their own village with real needs that will help their direct families.

There you go again! What makes you think we are not already involved in these things? The fact that people do not go on the Internet everyday to write about what they have done for their families does not mean they are not doing anything. Many diaspora Cameroonians I know are quietly undertaking a lot of projects to improve the lot of their family members or their village community back at home. At the same time, they can afford to be very vocal about desiring significant improvements in the conduct of public affairs at the national level. These two approaches are not mutually exclusive, you know.

The needs here are simple and require little investment of time or energy. There is always a need for another classroom, a small bridge, a farm to market road, an old car to be used as an ambulance, a grinder for a women's group, a scholarship for a child and so on.

Just in case you missed them, let me remind you of a few instances of a "little investment of time or energy" by the Camnet community. In 1996 a successful drive was launched to collect and transport books from abroad to the University of Buea in Cameroon. In 1997 a successful fund-raising campaign was undertaken to support a needy school in the district of Ngomo in Cameroon. In 1998 the North-West Provincial Academy was launched right here on Camnet to provide scholarships to deserving Cameroonian students. On numerous occasions, some Camnetters have posted requests for assistance on behalf of specific communities in Cameroon, and they have generally received a positive response. In light of all the foregoing and more, I don't think we need the patronising attitude.

Please act.

Obviously, Mike, we are acting. We are also talking. That, to me, is the sign of a healthy community.

Best regards.

Mola Njoh Endeley.

****

"The Biya Germ In Us"

Introduction

To close this chapter, I would like to share an exchange I had with other Camnetters regarding the fundamental nature, or essence, of the Cameroonian. Some of my interlocutors suggested that despite all the criticisms we direct at the régime, we are no different from Paul Biya and that, if given a chance, we would probably run and ruin the country in the same way as Biya has done. According to them, there is no point clamouring for change at the helm of the Cameroonian State, for we will merely end up "replacing one Biya with another Biya" since "we all have the Biya germ in us."

My response below is in the form of a political parody and should not be taken too literally. In essence, I am postulating that if it is in fact true that each and every Cameroonian is a repository for "the Biya germ", then it would require an extraordinary measure, such as the intervention of a "witch doctor," to rid us of the germ. I further postulate that since those who have ruined Cameroon have so far been males, it may perhaps not be a bad idea to consider entrusting our fate to competent females.

On August 8, 1998, Christmas Atem Ebini wrote:

[...]

The point I am making is that as Cameroonians, we all have the Biya germ in us and until we get cured of the Biya germ in us, we might still find ourselves replacing one Biya with another Biya and the circle would continue.

[...]

we are all ineffective with the Biya disease and until we get rid of the disease, we would always be Biyas at heart.

[...]

Biya and the CPDM are the results of our problem, not the problem itself. They are the curse on us for our sins and until we truly repent and cleanse ourselves as a people, we would always have curses and other Biyas.

Date: Sat, 8 Aug 1998 16:54:07 -0400
Sender: CAMNET
From: Isaac Endeley
Subject: **"The Biya Germ In Us"**

My Fellow Camnetters:

I need a volunteer, preferably of the female persuasion, to come over next weekend to help me get rid of "the Biya germ" in me. I'm at my wits' end, overwhelmed by more than my fair share of this terrible ailment, "the Biya disease". It's killing me. Are there any "witch doctors" or sorceresses in the house? Please respond. You will be very handsomely rewarded ($$$:-) :-) :-))

In anticipation,
Mola Njoh Endeley

****

Date: Tue, 11 Aug 1998 01:58:55 -0400
Sender: CAMNET
From: Isaac Endeley
Subject: Re: "Biya germ"

Dear Lilian:

Thanks for your reaction to the plea for help. But it feels odd to be addressed indirectly (in the third person) rather than directly (in the second person). However, Counsel, in keeping with the spirit of your cross-examination, Mola will endeavour (a la Bob Dole) to respond in the third person ;-)

You wrote:
On reading this first sentence one, being of the "female" persuasion", begins to feel rather good that Mola thinks so highly of one's "species" that he thinks only we can cure him of this "Biya Germ".

44

Your first impressions are correct here: Mola does indeed think very highly of Camnet women in particular and Cameroonian women in general. He holds them in higher esteem than he does their male counterparts. That is a fact. (At least the women are not responsible for the ruining of Mola's native country!)

Then Mola goes and spoils it all in his next sentence, which reads thus: "Are there any "witch doctors" or sorceresses in the house?"

This is a genuine request for assistance. Mola has already tried some of the other forms and sources of healing, but none of them yielded any tangible results. He hopes that, once again, a woman can succeed where many men have failed.

Am I to understand Mola thinks we are all "witches and sorceresses"?

No, Lilian. Mola does not think you are ALL witches and sorceresses. He was merely asking if ANY of you are. When Mola isn't sure of something, he prefers to ASK.

What about us females who may also be infected with this "Biya germ" and need a cure. Who do we turn Mola?

Mola recommends that you also turn to female "healers". There is ample evidence that the men are incapable of curing Mola's country and its citizens of "the Biya germ".

Finally, Mola hopes he has not dug himself further into the grave with this feeble attempt at a response. Meanwhile, he's still hurting and hoping to hear from potential female healers very soon ;-)

Ciao,

Mola Njoh Endeley.

45

Chapter II

On The Anglophone Problem

Kamerun and the League of Nations

Introduction

One of the perennial topics of discussion on Camnet was the issue of the status of the Anglophone minority in Cameroon. Although the Anglophones and Francophones on the forum tended to have similar views on most of the pertinent issues and often cooperated on a variety of projects initiated on Camnet, one area on which they generally failed to see things from each other's perspective was the so-called Anglophone problem. To many Francophones, the Anglophone problem is no different from all the other problems facing the country, including corruption, poverty, rigged elections, dilapidated infrastructure, a poor health care system, etc. To many Anglophones, however, the problem has its roots in Cameroon's colonial history and is much more significant that any of those other issues.

In this part of the publication I have attempted to compile a representative sample of my e-mail contributions on this subject and I hope the reader will emerge with a clearer picture of the larger issues involved. I start with an attempt to set the historical record straight before delving into a proper definition of the problem, followed by matters of personal experience and opinion.

On May 21, 1999, Kamguia Mu Fedjo' wrote: [See English translation in footnote]

Germain-Blaise a levé un coin de voile extrêmement lourd de conséquences en revenant à la racine historique du pays dont nous nous réclamons.

47

Effectivement, le Kamerun "allemand" fut saisi comme butin de guerre et confié à la France et à l'Angleterre par la Société des Nations, pour en prendre soin jusqu'au jour de l'indépendance, et non pour le diviser en deux états comme cela a été le cas, illégalement de par les normes internationales. Le Kamerun devait accéder à l'indépendance en un Bloc. Au lieu de cela, l'un de ces voyous, "Mother England" (voir ci-après), non content de nous avoir divisé en Francophones et Anglophones, a poussé l'effronterie à une partition du Kamerun sous son contrôle entre le Nigeria et "La République". Ce même voyou est à l'origine de la rébellion d'une province de l'Irak (Koweït) contre la patrie, et bien de misères dans le monde. C'est par la force des armes que les USA ont dit non à ce même voyou en 1776.

L'argument selon lequel le Kamerun est un et indivisible a un fondement historique incontournable. Comme l'a si bien dit Ndzie, ce que la France et l'Angleterre sont venus faire et ont laissé en place, c'est du bordel. Quelqu'un a récemment évoqué l'un de ces voyous coloniaux avec le vocable de "Mother England", sur ce réseau. J'en étais resté éberlué. J'espère que "Mother England" n'a pas complètement empoisonné l'esprit d'une partie du Kamerun. Je vois d'ici les rires moqueurs de ces racistes prenant leur thé à Trafalgar Square et écoutant un nègre parler de "Mother England". Comme les Français s'esclaffaient devant le spectacle ridicule de Jean Bedel Bokassa de Centrafrique pleurant la mort de "Papa De Gaulle".[3]

---

[3] By referring to the historical roots of the country we claim as ours, Germain-Blaise [Ndzié] has raised an issue with very serious consequences. In effect, "German" Kamerun was seized as the spoils of war and entrusted by the League of Nations to France and England for safekeeping until independence, and not to divide into two states, illegally and contrary to international standards, as was the case here. Kamerun was supposed to gain independence as a bloc. Instead, one of these thug, "Mother England" (see below), not satisfied with having divided us between Francophones and Anglophones, added insult to injury by dividing the part of Kamerun under its control between Nigeria and "La République". This same thug is also responsible for the rebellion of a province of Iraq (namely Kuwait) against the Iraqi nation, as well as for many other causes of misery around the world. Even the USA had to use military force against this same thug in 1776.

Date: Mon, 24 May 1999 06:48:28 +0200
Sender: CAMNET
From: Isaac Endeley
Subject: **Re: Le Kamerun et la SDN**

Hello again, KMF and Germain-Blaise:

Just ten quick points about the colonial history of Southern Cameroons.

1) The German "protectorate" of Kamerun, established in 1884, was overrun by the "Allied" forces in 1915-1916, with the French attacking from *l'Afrique équatoriale française* on the east and the British attacking from Nigeria on the west.

2) The two victorious powers agreed to share the spoils inequitably in Kamerun, with the British making up for the difference elsewhere, particularly in Tanganyika in East Africa.

3) As a consequence, the Brits took control of two non-contiguous strips of territory --Northern Cameroons and Southern

---

The assertion that Kamerun is one and indivisible has an indisputable historical basis. As Ndzie has stated so eloquently, what France and England came and did and then left behind is a real mess. Someone recently used the term "Mother England" to describe one of these colonial thug on this forum. I was stunned. I hope "Mother England" has not completely poisoned the minds of one part of Kamerun. I can just imagine the mocking laughter of those racists as they sip their tea at Trafalgar Square and listen to Negroes talk of "Mother England". Similarly, the French laughed at the ridiculous spectacle of Jean-Bedel Bokassa of Central Africa mourning the death of "Daddy De Gaulle".

Cameroons -- with a huge chunk of French-controlled territory (corresponding approximately to the present-day Adamawa and Northern provinces) in-between.

4) The two "Cameroons" territories under British control were governed separately as part of the Nigerian Federation. Within Southern Cameroons itself, there were two distinct provinces: the Bamenda Province (today's North-west) and the Cameroons Province (present-day South-west, approximately).

5) The League of Nations (*'Société des Nations'*, or SDN, in French) was established after the Versailles Treaty of 1919. It gave the British and the French a "mandate" to govern (or exploit) the conquered territories, but never claimed to be an advocate for their independence.

6) It was only after the United Nations Organisation was set up in 1945, and the Trusteeship system was established in 1946, that the question of independence became an issue. As the struggle gathered momentum in the 1950s, various proposals were advanced.

7) Whereas the French found their portion of Cameroun to be viable as an independent nation, the British deemed each of their non-contiguous territories to be insufficiently endowed to go solo. (Oil was yet to be discovered!)

8) The outcome was that each territory was given a choice between two limited options (essentially a choice between a rock and a hard place): Join Nigeria or join French Cameroun! The plebiscite, backed by the UN, was held on 11 February 1961.

9) By a vote of 232,000 to 93,000, Northern Cameroons decided to join the Nigerian Federation.* This happened on the 1st of October 1961.

10) By a vote of 140,000 to 98,000, Southern Cameroons agreed to join French Cameroun.* Meanwhile, a Constitutional Conference was held at Foumban in July 1961 to determine the shape of the union. It was decided that the new Cameroonian nation would be a federation comprising two states: British Southern Cameroons would become West Cameroon while French Cameroun would become East Cameroon. This happened on the 1st of October 1961.

The rest, as they say, is history.

A plus, mes compatriotes !

Mola Njoh Endeley.

(* Source: *"Chronologie politique africaine"*, Paris, *Fondation nationale des sciences politiques, 2e année, no. 1, janvier-février 1961, page 2.*)

****

What is the Anglophone Problem?

Date: Wed, 16 Apr 1997 00:19:37 -0400
Sender: CAMNET
From: Isaac Endeley
Subject: **What is the Anglophone Problem?**

What Is The Anglophone Problem?

A Minimalist Definition

The Anglophone problem is essentially a certain degree of unease and discomfort at the way government business and public affairs are being conducted under the present (predominantly

Francophone) government of Cameroon. Most Anglophones who have had any kind of contact with the country's institutions come out feeling cheated, even abused. The Anglophone problem is basically a matter of way of life. The degree of discontent and dissatisfaction will obviously vary with individual experience, but the underlying truth remains universal to all Anglophones.

As we all know, Cameroon is a truly variegated country with all sorts of social, economic and political cleavages between its different constituent parts. Among the most prominent dichotomies are those between the Northerners and the Southerners; between Christians and Muslims; between tradition and modernisation; between rural and urban populations; between the rich and the poor; between the young and the old; between the powerful and the weak; between males and females; and, of course, between the various ethnic groups as well as between supporters of different political tendencies.

It is my contention here that of all the markers distinguishing one group of Cameroonians from the next, by far the most significant is the linguistic dichotomy, the cleavage separating the English-speaking minority from the French-speaking majority. I believe this to be the case because the Anglophone/Francophone divide transcends ethnicity, social class, political persuasion, gender, age and religion, among other factors. This question touches not merely on the distribution of political power and wealth but, more importantly, on the way the societies are structured; the way the people are raised and educated; their relationship with their government and its institutions; the way justice is administered; and the world view of the people.

While I concede that it is a real pity to be debating on the relative merits of different colonial masters (since the one is necessarily just as bad as the other), I also think it would be foolhardy to attempt to overlook the impact that colonialism has had on us. The legacy bequeathed to us by both the British and the French during the 45 years or so (1916-1960/61) that they administered their respective Mandated and Trust Territories continues to have a major influence on our lives even today. The [official] languages we speak, the literature we read, the culture we acquire, or some of the philosophies we adopt, are all strongly influenced by our colonial heritage. The intention of the present contribution is not to claim that life in the former Southern Cameroons (later West Cameroon) was a bed of roses but, rather, that things were done DIFFERENTLY there.

West of the Mungo River, Anglophones learn to read and write in the English language; they are taught that all are equal before the law; that an accused person is considered innocent until proven guilty; that the police cannot (or should not) arrest anyone or search their home without a warrant; that torture should not be a part of the administration of justice; that the government is there to serve the people, and not vice versa; that government should be broken down to the smallest possible unit (as in a federation) in order to bring it closer to the people; that diversity should be celebrated rather than scorned; that respect for others is the cornerstone of a civil society; that freedom of expression --including the expression of dissent-- should be constitutionally guaranteed; and that the government should always maintain a dialogue with the governed.

Yet once Anglophones come into any form of contact with the central government located in Yaoundé or any of its appendages, they realize that all of this might as well have been a dream. For not only do the administrators (from the President of the Republic down to the *Préfets*, *Sous-Préfets*, etc.) refuse to speak the official language of the former Southern Cameroons, but Anglophone Cameroonians are also told in no uncertain terms that they are second-class citizens in their own country. Among Francophone Cameroonians (and increasingly among Anglophones, too), the world "Anglo" is used as an insult: it is synonymous with "backward," "uncivilised," "inconsequential," and what have you? It did not help matters that the 1972 Constitution clearly stated that only its French version was authentic; nor is it any consolation that all official documents are drafted and promulgated in French, then (poorly) translated into English only as an afterthought. The series of attempts by the Yaoundé government to eliminate all the institutions with which Anglophone Cameroonians are familiar and comfortable (e.g., the GCE, RSA and City & Guilds exams) and to ASSIMILATE the minority into the majority clearly demonstrate the perceived bad faith of the Francophone regime. This is what is often meant by the term "marginalisation" of the Anglophones.

In my estimation, the vast majority of Anglophone Cameroonians actually enjoy being Cameroonian; and they are not asking to become the president of the country or to be appointed minister of this or that. All they want is a chance to manage their own local affairs; a chance to feel that they belong, so that when they walk into a post office to buy postage stamps, the clerk does not ask them, "*Stamp c'est quoi ?*" (This actually happened to me in 1984!) At the very least, they need to be governed by people who speak the same language as they do, both literally and figuratively.

Some of our Francophone brethren have demonstrated an alarming level of naiveté by attempting to argue that there is no Anglophone problem. They maintain instead that there is only a Cameroonian problem, of which Paul Biya is the incarnation. Well, while recognising that President Biya is indeed a Cameroonian problem, I think we need to bear in mind that he is not the only one. The Anglophone problem existed well before Mr. Biya came to power and, if the present structures and institutions persist, it may continue to exist even after he leaves office. The issue at stake here is not a person, but a set of structures and institutions that favour one aspect of our dual heritage to the detriment of the other. It is the simple refusal to acknowledge this problem that has pushed some Anglophones to espouse extremism, and the recent waves of violence surrounding the Easter 1997 season should have awakened all sleeping dogs.

The point bears repeating: the Anglophone problem is essentially a certain degree of unease and discomfort at the way public affairs are managed under the present (predominantly Francophone) government of Cameroon. It is the product of a high level of frustration with the country's current institutional arrangements. Many Anglophones would rather return to the type of institutions with which they feel comfortable.

Any measure of recognition of this basic fact on the part of the Francophone government would go a long way towards healing the wounds. But in the final analysis, perhaps a devolutionary political dispensation, as in a federation where different people manage their own local affairs, would be the best solution.

As for the number of units in such a federation, the current ten provinces might not be a bad starting point.

Enough said.

Isaac Njoh Endeley

****

The Fatal Errors of the Foumban Conference of July 1961

Introduction

Following the UN-backed plebiscite of February 1961, in which the majority of voters in the then-Southern Cameroons opted to attain independence by reuniting with French Cameroun rather than by remaining in the Nigerian Federation, the leaders of the two Cameroons met in Foumban in July 1961 to discuss the terms of a newly reunited country's Constitution. The circumstances and substance of the Constitutional Conference, as well as the perceived good faith –or bad faith– of the delegates, has been the subject of much discussion on Camnet and in other Cameroonian fora.

In August 1997 one experienced and knowledgeable Camnetter wrote a lengthy article in which he catalogued what he viewed as the fatal errors committed by the conference participants. In particular, he argued that since the former Southern Cameroons was not a sovereign or independent nation, its Premier, Mr. John Ngu Foncha, was not qualified to negotiate with President Ahmadou Ahidjo whose country, La République du Cameroun, was already sovereign and independent. Instead, he suggests that the United Nations and the

United Kingdom should have been the ones negotiating on behalf of Southern Cameroonians.

In my response below, I attempt to show, by reference to international law and practice, that the gentleman's argument was flawed and that the Union between East and West Cameroon was properly consummated and has become an irreversible reality.

Date: Thu, 21 Aug 1997 02:16:07 -0400
Sender: CAMNET
From: Isaac Endeley
Subject: **Re: The Fatal Errors of the Foumban Conference of July 1961**

On August 15, 1997, N.N. Susungi wrote:

(i) Fatal Error Committed by the UN and the UK.

Given the fact at the time of Foumban negotiations John Ngu Foncha was only the Prime Minister of a UN Trust Territory (whose sovereignty was still in the custody of the United Kingdom), while President Ahidjo was already the President of an independent and sovereign state, the proper legal implementation of UN Resolution 1608 of April 1961 demanded that the negotiations in Foumban on the constitutional future of the Southern Cameroons should have taken place between President Ahidjo and the duly mandated representative of the United Kingdom and not with John Ngu Foncha.

Dear Dr. Susungi:

I have perused your many contributions to Camnet with a great deal of interest and I admire your penchant for debate and dialogue. That said, I find it very easy to refute your entire argument in this case because it is hinged on a faulty premise, encapsulated in the segment reproduced above. Allow me to explain.

From the vantage point of International Relations and International Law, it is perfectly legitimate for one actor to delegate authority to another. Hence, just as the United Nations could ENTRUST the administration of the Trust Territory of the Southern Cameroons to the Government of the United Kingdom, so, too, could the latter DELEGATE such authority to the duly elected Government of Prime Minister John Ngu Foncha. The same principle applies when it comes to negotiating international treaties. After all, the Southern Cameroonians themselves were the ones who would subsequently have to cohabit with their cousins east of the Mungo River. So who better to negotiate the terms of such cohabitation than those with a direct interest in the outcome of the negotiations? The British were, therefore, acting well within the compass of established international practice by asking the democratically elected Government of the Southern Cameroons to represent its own people's aspirations. Contrary to your assertion, reunification DID indeed take place after midnight on September 30, 1961, and this is borne out by the international recognition the reunified territory has since enjoyed. Any attempt to deny this is simply wishful thinking.

Where the problem arose was in the negotiating skills of the Southern Cameroonian team at the Conference (and I think John Mbaku makes this point very, very eloquently). For all their intellectual baggage, they relied too heavily on their own judgement of President Ahidjo's character and allowed themselves to be outsmarted in Foumban. They took Mr. Ahidjo at face value and failed to push hard enough for genuine constitutional guarantees. Furthermore, while it is true that Ahidjo benefited immensely from a horde of sagacious French advisers, it is no less true that the Southern Cameroonian delegation could have fared much better were it not riven with internecine rivalries, tribalism and personality conflicts. There is no doubt that gross injustices have been perpetrated as a result of the unsatisfactory outcome of that Constitutional Conference, but that can hardly be imputed to the UN or to the UK.

To state the point differently, would you be leveling the same charges against the UN and the UK today had the Foncha Government managed to wrest significant concessions from Mr. Ahidjo at that Conference? I think not. And therein lies the fallacy of your argument.

Yes, Anglophone Cameroonians were gravely wronged at the Foumban Constitutional Conference and we have every right to seek redress. But if we are going to play the 'blame game,' then I suggest we start by blaming ourselves. The old tactic of attributing all of our inadequacies to the colonial master no longer holds much sway.

An alternative option available to us is to find ways of amending the Constitution so that it reflects the genuine aspirations of all Cameroonians and ensures full participation. This is the route I prefer to go. No use crying over spilt milk.

Catch you on the rebound,

Mola Njoh Endeley.

****

The Last Attorney-General

Introduction

I had the good fortune in December of 1996 of meeting Justice Emmanuel Koffi Mensah, the last individual to hold the portfolio of Attorney-General of West Cameroon. He graciously granted a request for an audio- and video-recorded interview and my colleagues and I proceeded to discuss a wide variety of issues with him. I subsequently prepared a written summary of the interview, which I posted via e-mail on Camnet in December 1996 and again in July 1997. As the e-mail format of discussions on Camnet did not easily lend itself to a verbatim transcription of the interview, including all the questions asked and responses given, it was unnecessary to prepare a more detailed report of the interview.

Date: Mon, 28 Jul 1997 13:28:08 -0400
Sender: CAMNET
From: Isaac Endeley
Subject: **The Last Attorney-General**

Hi, folks:

This biographical note on Justice Koffi Mensah was first posted on Camnet in December 1996. But at that time, many of you might have been on vacation and others may not yet have been subscribed to the network. I am therefore taking the liberty of reproducing the note, albeit with slight modifications, in the hope of eliciting some kind of reaction, particularly from older Camnetters or from all those who may have known the former Attorney-General in one way or another.

Few Cameroonians, whether Anglophone or Francophone, seem to remember that there once existed in the former federated state of West Cameroon the portfolio of Attorney-General, the cabinet equivalent of what we now know as the Minister of Justice. Probably fewer still will remember Justice Emmanuel Kofi Mensah, the last Attorney-General of West Cameroon. Once a prominent political and judiciary figure in Cameroon, he was forced by the excesses of the Ahidjo regime to go into exile in 1971. During a recent private visit to the home of his daughter, son-in-law and grandchildren in Chicago, the good Judge was gracious enough to grant Dibussi Tande and myself an extensive interview. (The full text of that interview has been published elsewhere.) A video recording was also made, courtesy of Gervase Ndoko. Meanwhile, here's a brief summary of the encounter.

Emmanuel Kofi Mensah was born in Victoria in 1938 and raised in Buea. He attended St. Joseph's College, Sasse and distinguished himself not only by his brilliant academic career, but also by his athletic ability. He boasts of having been the goalkeeper of the college football team and of being fondly referred to by his erstwhile schoolmates by the nickname "Water Snake". He graduated from Sasse in 1955 and was admitted to King's College, University of London, where he studied law. Thereafter, he underwent a period of pupilage in London, during which he established his credentials as an outstanding constitutional lawyer.

He returned home to Buea in 1960 to work in the Legal Department of the Southern Cameroonian and, later, West Cameroonian governments. He participated as a Legal Adviser in the 1961 Foumban Constitutional Conference that led to the reunification of English-speaking West Cameroon and French-speaking East Cameroon. (By the way, he considers West Cameroon to have been 'sold out' at that Conference.) His entire career path presented him with a unique vantage position from which to observe and influence the metamorphosis of the Cameroonian Federation.

In 1962, Kofi Mensah again went to Europe, this time to earn a Master's degree in law at Queen's University in Belfast, Northern Ireland. He returned home in 1964 to resume his judiciary functions. So great were his accomplishments and so brilliant was his intellect that, at the relatively tender age of 26 years, he was appointed Assistant Attorney-General of West Cameroon. He held that position until 1966 when he became a Chief Magistrate and then spent the next two years in the field, serving successively in Bamenda, Kumba and Banso. In 1968, he became the Attorney-General of West Cameroon, the highest-ranking judiciary official in the territory and the custodian of the constitutional rights of all Anglophone Cameroonians.

He describes the ensuing period as an interesting time, characterized by the difficulty of marrying the British legal and political systems of West Cameroon to the French ones inherited by East Cameroon after independence. He also cites a number of ideological differences with the Ahidjo regime, particularly his opposition to the president's propensity to use decrees to override or amend constitutional provisions. Consequently, he found himself at loggerheads with the president on more than a few occasions. The final straw, he says, came in 1971 when President Ahidjo decided to abolish the post of Attorney-General of West Cameroon and to create, in its stead, that of Legal Adviser to the President. Disagreeing in principle with the president, he no longer felt he could perform his duties freely within such a system and became unsure even about his own personal safety. That was when he decided to go into voluntary exile.

Since 1971, Justice Kofi Mensah has been living in Ghana, where he has many relatives and friends. Before retiring a short while ago, he worked as a Judge of the Ghanaian Supreme Court and has always enjoyed a close personal relationship with President Jerry Rawlings. Although he has managed to visit Cameroon in recent years, he says he still misses his friends and relatives living there. Among the most striking changes he has observed are the effects of the discovery of petroleum on the Limbe (Victoria) area and the evolution of the Cameroonian political scene. He says he still follows Cameroonian affairs on a regular basis.

During our interview, the judge made insightful comments about the concepts of good governance, democracy, federalism, ethnicity, tribalism, and nationalism, with regard not only to Cameroon, but to the entire African continent as well. He also volunteered some interesting ideas on how the OAU could be rendered more effective.

Justice Kofi Mensah still dreams of returning to Cameroon for good. "Home is always home," he says.

Peace to all,

Mola Njoh Endeley.

****

The Last Attorney-General

Introduction

I received a good number of responses to the e-mail on Justice Mensah, and since most of them were positive and not at all controversial, they did not generally elicit from me any reactions worth reproducing here. However, one fellow Camnetter made the following observation, to which I responded as indicated below.

On July 29, 1997, Steve Andoseh wrote:

It occurred to me in reading this piece that Ghana must have been some kind of haven for political exiles in the late '50s and '60s. One of my distant relatives who was involved with Ntumazah and the 'One Kamerun' movement betook himself to Ghana after he ran into political complications at home. A host of UPC militants also made for Ghana in fleeing Ahidjo's persecution. What was so conducive about Ghana? I'd like to know the forces that were at work then.

Date: Thu, 31 Jul 1997 13:30:51 -0400
Sender: CAMNET
From: Isaac Endeley
Subject: **Re: The Last Attorney-General**

Hi, Steve:

I believe the primary explanation for this is the ideological affinity between Ghanaian President Kwame Nkrumah and other African Marxist-Leninists. Nkrumah's highly publicised dream of creating a 'United States of Africa' (and an 'African High Command') based on the Soviet model rendered Ghana into a singular pole of attraction for many Black Africans with a socialist/communist bent. Between 1957 and 1966 when he was overthrown, Nkrumah was continuously being accused by the leaders of other independent

African nations, including President Ahidjo of Cameroon, of fomenting plots and *coups d'état* against them. Cold War politics were very much at work at the time, and Nkrumah, together with Guinea's Sékou Touré, took a lot of pride in harbouring the so-called African revolutionaries.

In Justice Koffi Mensah's case, however, I think the main reason he sought refuge in Ghana in 1971 is kinship rather than ideology. Although he was born and raised in Cameroon, his father hailed from Ghana and he still has many relatives living there. (I seem to recall that he even hinted during our interview that he had some kind of blood relationship with President Rawlings, but I'm not absolutely certain.)

Peace to you,

Mola Njoh Endeley.

****

Chapter III

On "Character" Vs "Institutions"

"Character" vs. "Institutions"

Introduction

In our efforts to build a strong, stable, responsible and responsive State in Cameroon should we accord the priority to identifying leaders with "good character" or should we place the emphasis on building viable "institutions" that can withstand the test of time? This is one of the questions over which members of the Camnet forum conducted numerous debates through the years. Each side of the debate had solid support from thoughtful persons making insightful contributions backed by sound logic and concrete experience. At the same time, each side was firmly entrenched in its position and, to the best of my recollection, unanimity was never achieved. Nor was that the objective.

On my part, as the reader will see, I have consistently subscribed to the view that a solid institutional framework is much more important than the character of the leaders. This view is supported by many historical and contemporary examples, of which I need to cite only one from each extreme. On the one hand, the Clinton-Lewinsky saga in the USA proves that despite the admittedly flawed character of a leader, where solid institutions exist, the nation will not suffer. On the other hand, the spectacular failure of Prime Minister Peter Musonge in Cameroon proves that despite the upright character of a leader, the nation will continue to suffer in the absence of adequate institutions. In the next few pages I present excerpts of lengthy debates over the issue of "character" vs. "institutions". As the reader will see, some of the exchanges became quite personal and highly emotionally charged.

Date: Mon, 24 May 1999 06:48:10 +0200
Sender: CAMNET
From: Isaac Endeley
Subject: **"Character" vs "Institutions"**

Dear Pierre Faa and Pierre Kamguia:

Pardon the pun, brothers, but over the years I've been pining for a chance to kill two birds with one stone :-) :-) (*faire d'une "pierre" deux coups !*)

The current debate on whether a leader's moral character should take precedence over the nation's institutional framework, or vice versa, is a perennial one here on Camnet. I'm sure you're both familiar with my position by now. Sadly, none of your suggestions so far in the discussion has given me any cause to modify my stance. If anything, much of what you've stated in your recent postings appears to buttress the opposing view. Let me demonstrate this by commenting on excerpts from your texts.

Pierre Faa wrote:

11) Benin: Maybe the only success story so far. And this is more related to change in mentalities than change in institutions... Kerekou for example is a different man today than he was ten, fifteen years ago...

I beg to differ. The Republic of Benin is one of the few success stories on the African continent today precisely because it undertook a radical transformation of its institutional framework in the late 1980s and early 1990s. Short of playing God, there is no possible way of verifying that President Mathieu Kérékou's character has changed fundamentally from what it was in the days of his Marxist-Leninist dictatorship to something else at the present time. What is certain is that his country today has new, transparent institutions, designed in consultation with all the relevant segments of the population. The new structures effectively restrict opportunism and discourage the

66

desire to cheat. As such, even after losing at the previous presidential election, Mr Kérékou was able to come back and defeat Mr Nicéphore Soglo the next time around without either one of them complaining of fraud. That is not a measure of character. It is a measure of the strength of institutions and the level of faith they inspire in the people.

Pierre Kamguia Mu Fedjo (KMF) wrote:

Les exemples sud-africain et béninois sur notre continent, américain au-delà de l'Atlantique, semblent indiquer qu'au départ, des hommes de caractère (Mandela, Washington, Jefferson, Madison) et un changement de caractère de l'homme (Kérékou) font plus que des théories universitaires couchées dans un livre.[4]

Here, once again, the point is being missed by a wide margin. George Washington, Thomas Jefferson and James Madison are being celebrated today not for their moral rectitude or their flawless character. (Recent research, with some help from Hollywood, has demystified a lot of things about them as individuals.) Rather, they are being celebrated today for having had the foresight to create solid institutions that have withstood the test of time. Witness the recent impeachment of President William Jefferson Clinton (a confessed flawed character) and the strength of institutions that frustrated attempts by petty partisan politics to triumph over the will of the people. In President Nelson Mandela's case as well, the lasting legacy will likely be strength of the "colour-blind and colourless" institutions he has striven to erect for his country, rather than any more-or-less subjective assessment of his character.

---

[4] The cases of South Africa and Benin on our continent, and America across the Atlantic, seem to indicate that at the onset men of character (such as Mandela, Washington, Jefferson, Madison) and a change of man's character (Kérékou) have a greater impact that university theories laid down in textbooks.

Finally, I've taken the liberty of reproducing below a response I sent to another Camnetter when this issue was discussed here a little over a year ago. I would be interested in seeing how either of you, Pierre and Pierre, can counter the examples from both extremes. Add to that the fact that, under the same "moral" leadership, the U.S. is currently seeing its best economic performance in over a generation whereas our beloved Cameroon has since earned the dubious distinction of being classified as the world's most corrupt nation!

Bye for now.

Mola Njoh Endeley.

****

Date: Thu, 30 Apr 1998 23:08:11 -0400
Sender: CAMNET
From: Isaac Endeley
Subject: **Re: Self-examination**

On April 30, 1998, Coz Kange wrote:

An Institution in itself cannot exist as an entity until it is embodied by one or more Individuals. It is in semblance to the Institution of life in a human body - - remove the life and the Institution crumbles to dust.

Hello, Coz:

I don't think any of those involved in this debate so far has made the claim that institutions can, or ought to, function without people. I believe the argument has been about whether the priority should be accorded to the character of the leaders or to the nature of the nation's laws and institutions. The ideal, of course, should include the best of both components. However, this is not an ideal world.

68

Therefore, I tend to agree with Steve Andoseh, Aristide Tchamdjou, John Mbaku, Lyombe Eko and Mana Titamboh, among others, that good laws and solid institutions are our best guarantee against corruption and the abuse of power. To illustrate my point, allow me to cite two concrete instances, one each from the opposite extremes.

In the USA, where you currently reside, President Bill Clinton is widely acknowledged to be of questionable moral character. Indeed, as you and I are aware, there is no end to the queue of litigants vying to pursue him for this or that transgression. Yet, due to the strength of that country's institutions, including an independent judiciary, a transparent electoral process, and a free press, the state's activities have not suffered any significant setback. Because America's laws were properly designed and involve the active participation of the governed, they are eminently enforceable. In general, people seem to realise that the laws in place are in their best interest. Perhaps more importantly, Americans know there is a process through which such laws can be amended or repealed should they become obsolete. These factors alone constitute a sufficient incentive for compliance. While the US is far from being an *"El Dorado"*, it is doing very well in virtually every domain and continues to attract the best and the brightest from the world over. **The leader's character is largely irrelevant!**

Par contre, in Cameroon, from whence you hail, President Paul Biya was generally believed to be morally upright when he acceded to power in 1982. His credo of "rigour and moralisation" was highly touted as the antidote to our nation's ailments. Yet, in the absence of good laws and solid institutions, the President's own acolytes (e.g. the notorious Andze Tsoungui) were among the first to flout his moral injunction. As Lyombe and Steve have already pointed out, Cameroon has regressed considerably in the intervening years. In the absence of good laws and institutions, the populace remains subjected to the whims and caprices of the ruling clique. The average Cameroonian has no incentive to comply with the prevailing laws and feels powerless to effect any meaningful change. In light of the stiff sentence recently meted out to a journalist who merely questioned the state of the President's health, for instance, can you imagine the fate that would befall anyone who attempts to sue the head of state for anything? Without the proper institutions to protect them against arbitrary rule, Cameroonians in their numbers will continue to dream of making a permanent home elsewhere. **Laws and institutions do matter!**

Corruption is not a uniquely Cameroonian or African phenomenon. It is common to all human societies. Its prevalence in our society is best explained not by any moral shortcoming on our part, but by the absence of proper legal and institutional frameworks to reduce the temptation to cheat. "Self-examination" or introspection is always a good thing. However, what every nation needs in order to reduce the incidence of corruption and arbitrary rule is a set of viable laws and institutions.

(How such laws and institutions are designed and implemented is a whole different issue. In that regard, I found Asa'ah Nkohkwo's appeal for a "pragmatic" approach very cogent indeed. But I digress . . .)

Looking forward to pursuing the dialogue.

Warmest wishes,

Mola Njoh Endeley.

****

On May 25, 1999, Steve Andoseh wrote:

Let me make a suggestion. I think to proceed further each contributor in this debate should elaborate how he/she envisions a political transition playing out in Cameroon under a scenario that gives primacy to his/her position on this issue. Tell us, if you are a 'character' advocate for instance, how public policy may be conducted in Cameroon to ensure that good character holds sway, how such character may be cultivated and harvested, and the changes, if any, that must occur in the relevant milieux for your vision to take hold. The 'institution' advocate can do the same thing.

[...]

Any takers?

Hello, Steve:

Never one to pass up a challenge, I think I'm ready to fire the first salvo. Before that, however, I'd like to state that I think we've made significant progress in this discussion over the last couple of days. Some kind of consensus appears to be emerging and I want to commend both Faa and KMF for their constructive contributions.

I place myself firmly in what you may consider the institutionalist school of thought. (Surprise, surprise!) I believe good laws and solid institutions are *'sine qua non'* conditions for the development of a healthy body politic, a genuine civil society, the rule or law, the reduction of corruption, and the elimination of arbitrary government. If there is a consensus on this issue with the proponents of the other trends of thought, where we part company is on the preconditions for the establishment of such laws and institutions.

71

Whereas some seem to think these structures can only come about as a result of sacrifices from "people of character", I believe the same ends can be achieved through other means. Let me proceed here to briefly discuss a few of the latter.

* Mass education (as Djeukam Tchameni would put it) is one possibility. Provide the people with enough information about their rights and privileges, not forgetting their duties and obligations; raise their level of political consciousness; make them aware of the various alternatives to their current quagmire; and you can arrive at a "critical mass" -- the point where they start openly demanding a bigger bang for their buck (or their franc), regardless of the consequences. This gradualist approach should eventually lead to institutional reforms reflecting the people's true aspirations. The problem is that it might take too long.

* A civil disobedience campaign (not to be confused with a "ghost towns" operation). This assumes, obviously, that the people already have a sufficiently high level of consciousness. Get them to selectively target the prevailing laws and institutions that are not in the public interest, and then to work in a peaceful way to stifle same. Of course, someone will have to present a clear and universally accepted definition of the public interest. The problems here include the fact that symbolic and charismatic leaders are hard to come by, particularly in a diverse society like Cameroon, as well as the possibility that things could easily degenerate into violence.

* A propaganda assault. Pick on everything the incumbent government does and attempt to portray it in the worst possible light. Use subtle and subliminal advertising, but on a significantly large scale to influence public opinion both nationally and internationally. Make it imperative for the government to want to repair its tarnished image and hence to gradually make concessions. One difficulty with this method is that some leaders do not have a conscience ("*On s'en fout !*"). Therefore, positive results could be rare.

72

* A popular uprising, or a revolution. Convince the people that the last straw has just broken the camel's back (*"wata pass garri"*) and that they have already endured too much suffering. Let them know they had better seize their chance now or they will continue to be exploited by the ruling clique. This approach is not without its problems, as popular movements tend to turn into mob rule and physical violence could easily become widespread.

* I abhor military violence in politics, so I will not consider that option.

* I also have a loathing for the elitist option which suggests that "men of character" should get together and decide for the rest of us (as if the rest of us have no character)!

I'll pause here for now and let others have their take.

Peace.

Mola Njoh Endeley.

****

"Character" vs. "Institutions"

Introduction

As the debate progressed over time, participants would ask each other directly for clarification on certain issues. To their credit, most of those involved in the discourse never let matters degenerate into a personality conflict. However, this also means a few of those involved did let themselves get carried away by extraneous considerations. Moreover, as an illustration of the bilingual nature of the Camnet forum, some participants switched seamlessly back and forth between English and French. The exchange below is just one example of such bilingualism. I have chosen to leave the initial comments and responses in French but I have provided the English translations of both texts as footnotes.

Le 24 mai 1999, Mu Fedjo a écrit:

Je suppose que l'audience attend une réponse de moi, étant donne l'interpellation directe contenue dans le texte d'Isaac ci-dessous reproduit.

Je serai bref. Il me semble évident que de bonnes institutions sont indispensables pour assurer l'harmonie de l'exercice et du transfert du pouvoir. La question est, comment ces bonnes institutions naissent-elles ? C'est à ce niveau que ma réponse est: de la volonté de Bonnes Personnes. C'est pour cela que j'ai toujours pris soin de préciser qu'AU DEPART, il me semble que le caractère des hommes soit un ingrédient essentiel à l'adoption de bonnes institutions.

Pratiquement, qu'est-ce que cela veut dire ? Je ne sais pas comment boucler cette quadrature du cercle. Il faut des hommes vertueux pour dessiner un bon système sans pièges (les filous peuvent aussi dessiner un bon système, mais la tendance est pour eux de le truffer de pièges à exploiter par la suite), et if faut un bon système sans pièges pour forcer les hommes à se comporter honorablement.

You help me here.
Bonne journée.[5] KMF

---

[5] On 24 May 1999, Mu Fedjo wrote:

I suppose the readers are awaiting my response, since Isaac has mentioned my name directly in his mail.

I will be brief. It seems clear to me that good institutions are indispensable to ensuring harmony in the exercise and transfer of power. The question, then, is how are these good institutions created? My response here is the following: from the will of Good Persons. That is why I have always specified that it seems to me that IN THE BEGINNING men's character is essential to the establishment of good institutions.

Date: Wed, 26 May 1999 09:34:00 +0200
Sender: CAMNET
From: Isaac Endeley
Subject: **Re: "Character" vs "Institutions"**

Cher KMF,

Merci d'avoir pris le temps pour répondre à mes interrogations. Je suis soulagé de constater que l'on commence enfin à s'entendre sur certains éléments de base, à savoir, que de bonnes institutions sont nécessaires et indispensables à la gestion de l'État et au bon fonctionnement de la chose politique. Mais la question qui se pose par la suite, et à laquelle je ne prétends pas avoir la meilleure réponse, renvoie à la manière de faire naitre ces institutions. Il existe à ce propos deux hypothèses principales dont je vais tenter ici de résumer brièvement les grandes lignes.

D'une part, vous prétendez que des hommes de caractère, ou des personnes vertueuses, constituent un élément essentiel à la mise en place de ces institutions. Si tel est vraiment le cas, comment alors mesurer le caractère des gens ? Comment savoir si telle personne est de bonne volonté ou si telle autre est de mauvaise foi ? Il s'agirait dès lors de porter un jugement forcément subjectif sur les gens, ce qui pourrait conduire à des résultats arbitraires et aléatoires.

D'autre part, d'aucuns affirment que ces institutions devraient naitre de la volonté librement exprimée d'un peuple. Autrement dit, il faudrait au préalable que le peuple puisse articuler lui-même ses propres préférences quant à la forme des institutions à adopter. Ceci

---

In practical terms, what does this mean? I do not know how exactly to square this circle. It takes men of virtue to craft a good system without pitfalls (dishonest men can also design good systems, but they are more likely to insert shortcomings that they will later exploit), and it takes a good system without pitfalls to force men to behave honourably.

You help me here.

Have a nice day.

pourrait se faire de diverses manières, y compris l'éducation populaire, les campagnes de désobéissance civile, la propagande politique, et les soulèvements populaires.

Prétendre qu'il faudrait des gens de caractère pour décider à la place du peuple relève essentiellement de l'élitisme. C'est dire que le peuple est incapable de réfléchir et de connaitre ce qu'il veut; c'est dire qu'il lui faut toujours un "grand camarade" pour décider à sa place; c'est dire enfin que l'on méprise les populations !

Au plaisir de vous relire.[6]

---

[6] Dear KMF:

Thank you for taking the time to respond to my inquiry. I am relieved to note that we are finally beginning to agree on some fundamental points, namely that good institutions are necessary and indispensable for good governance and for the smooth functioning of a political system. However, the question that arises out of this, and to which I do not necessarily claim to have the best answer, relates to the manner of establishing such institutions. In that connection, there are two leading hypotheses whose broad outlines I will endeavour to summarise here.

On the one hand, you maintain that men of character, or people of virtue, are essential to the establishment of such institutions. If this is in fact the case, how would we determine people's character? How would we distinguish those with good intentions from those acting in bad faith? We would then be forced to make subjective judgements about people and this could lead to arbitrary and random results.

On the other hand, some people claim that solid institutions should flow naturally from the freely expressed will of the people. In other words, as a precondition the people must first be in a position to express their preferences regarding the types of institutions to adopt. There are different ways of doing this, including by mass education, civil disobedience campaigns, political propaganda, and popular uprisings.

The argument that men of character need to decide on behalf of the people strikes me as essentially an elitist view. It suggests that the people are incapable of thinking and of knowing what they want; it suggests that the people always need a "big brother" to decide for them; it also suggests disdain for the people!

****

On P. M. Musonge's Tenure

Introduction

The first two years of Mr. Peter Mafany Musonge's tenure as Prime Minister of Cameroon (September 1996 to September 1998) turned out to be a fantastic illustration of the limits of "good character" as a guarantor of good governance. At the time of his appointment, he was hailed as "a man of character" and a no-nonsense technocrat who would clean up the huge bureaucratic and institutional mess in Yaoundé and throughout Cameroon. Yet the reality of the situation turned out to be quite the opposite. For two consecutive years during Mr. Musonge's tenure, Transparency International, the self-appointed global monitor on fair business practices, ranked Cameroon as "the world's most corrupt country."

In an e-mail to the Camnet community in September 1998, I called for a reassessment of Mr. Musonge's performance in light of the high expectations at the time he had assumed office. In the end, I suggested that since his "good character" alone was not a sufficient criterion to improve the quality of people's lives, he should consider resigning. I received a lot of negative fallout for that suggestion, much of which is unfit for public consumption. Some of my critics took me to task for betraying my tribe; others concluded that my writings were the manifestation of a family feud between the Endeleys and the Musonges. In fact, I was even privately rebuked by some members of my own family for daring to criticise the Prime Minister publicly.

Looking forward to reading from you again.

The reality of the situation, however, is that in the absence of a solid institutional framework, even a morally upright and virtuous leader like Mr. Musonge is doomed to failure. I am pleased to report that amid the barrage of insults and criticism to which I was subjected, there also existed a few voices of reason that were able to clearly comprehend and articulate the essence of my position. I have taken the liberty of reproducing substantial segments of those contributions in this part of the book in support of my contention.

Date: Fri, 25 Sep 1998 01:53:21 -0400
Sender: CAMNET
From: Isaac Endeley
Subject: **Shouldn't Musonge Resign?**

Fellow Cameroonians:

This week marks the second anniversary of Mr. Peter Mafany Musonge's appointment as Prime Minister and Head of Government. His rise to the helm in September 1996 was highly touted by the CPDM's spin doctors as a possible antidote to our country's many ailments. He was hailed as a man of high integrity, morality and competence -- in much the same way as his current boss had been hailed 14 years before. Yet during Musonge's tenure Cameroon's international standing appears to have declined rather than improved. His widely publicised anti-corruption campaign, launched a few months ago, seems to have had effects quite different from what might have been expected.

Earlier this month, the United Nations Development Programme ranked Cameroon number 132 on its 'Human Development Index' listing. A few days ago, Transparency International labeled Cameroon the world's most corrupt country.

In the face of such overwhelming evidence of failure, shouldn't Musonge do the honourable thing and step down? How can he hope to lead trade missions abroad in the future and convince foreigners to invest in Cameroon? After two years in office, what can he boast of having accomplished? He has clearly not succeeded in having any significant impact on the sorry state of affairs in the country. Presiding over a dozen cabinet meetings a week and giving grandiloquent speeches are not enough. The people need concrete and tangible results.

I realise, of course, that the primary responsibility for our country's poor international (and national) standing lies squarely on the shoulders of our "leader", Paul Biya. But I'm sure you will agree with me that the man is beyond hope, beyond redemption. In all likelihood, we will just have to wait patiently for him to kick the bucket -- unless we can somehow precipitate his demise. Meanwhile, if a man like Musonge wishes to be remembered fondly by history, then perhaps this is the time for him to step aside. Or else he should stop pretending to be a saint.

I say he should resign. What do you say?

Best regards.

Mola Njoh Endeley.

****

Date:	Sat, 26 Sep 1998 19:16:46 -0400
Sender:	CAMNET
From:	Isaac Endeley
Subject:	**Re: Shouldn't Musonge Resign?**

Dear Emmanuel Mbesang:

By pure coincidence, the very same kind of response I was planning to send to you has already been written by Jude Anoma. I invite you to carefully re-read his piece.

Peace to you,

Mola Njoh Endeley.

****

Date:	*Sat, 26 Sep 1998 08:23:07 -0400*
Sender:	*CAMNET*
From:	*<jude.anoma@...>*
Subject:	**Re: Shouldn't Musonge Resign?**

As beautiful as [Mr. Emmanuel Mbesang's] posting is, I can't understand why it had to end the way it did. I was actually savoring the good points until I came to the part which dealt with Mola Endeley's tribe. Your insinuations, be they overt or subvert, are the weak points in an otherwise well-written piece, peppered by sound arguments and salient points. Why inject 'tribal' loyalties into this debate?Must it always revert to ethnic origins? Why place Mola Endeley in the unenviable position of 'damned if you do it and be damned if you don't?' If he had 'praised' Mr. Musonge, I am sure some would have said it is because he is Bakweri. Now that he castigates him or questions his stewardship, you question his loyalty. What is he supposed to be? A sheep? A blind person? A sycophant? A non-thinker?

Generally speaking, Mr. Musonge's stewardship is controvertible and no matter what side of the fence one finds oneself on, let's hope it's not influenced by one's tribal origins but by an independent ability to think and judge for oneself. This in itself is an attainable ideal which should be devoid of loyalties or non-salutary proclivities. Otherwise, how judicious would our conclusions be when they become tainted by 'outside' considerations?

****

80

Date: Sun, 27 Sep 1998 09:50:25 -0500
Sender: CAMNET
From: Sally N Woleta
Subject: **Re: Shouldn't Musonge Resign?**

[...]

Hello Mr. Bell,

Good day. Just like many others, I have been following your writings on this forum for quite a while now. With all due respect, I would like to say to you that if you do not have any relevant information or knowledge about a particular subject matter, it's okay to be a silent reader like some of us. As Mr. Asong puts it, "There is no logical connection between the cleanliness of a man's house and his effectiveness in office".

By the way, since Mr. Musonge is your HERO, can you please outline briefly for us what he has accomplished so far in office, for him to be that important to you? Or is it because you did see your face on his wall when (as you claim) you went over to his for some papers to be signed?

Just a point of correction: The person [Isaac Endeley] who asked the original question about Mr. Musonge is not from Bamenda.

Thanks and have a pleasant day.
Sally Woleta

****

On September 29, 1998, Steve Andoseh wrote:

Boy, the Musonge apologists would dearly love to make Endeley a Bamenda man, won't they? It would make everything perfectly easy for them. Heck some of them have gone ahead and MADE him an Abakwa man. Next thing he won't be Endeley anymore; he'd be Foncha (hey, Isaac Foncha, whatzup! Give me a holler). Never thought I'd live to see the day when an Endeley is confused for a Bamenda man. What's next, Biya a Bamileke? Ahidjo a Bulu? Soppo Priso a Hausa?

Kate, Sane, you may want to read a posting for CONTEXT. Isaac made it clear enough for the dispassionate reader.

- *Context: Mr. Musonge was widely held to be a man of integrity when he joined the government.*

- *Context: Mr. Musonge made the fight against corruption his highest priority.*

- *Context: During his tenure Cameroon has gone from the 5th most corrupt nation to THE most corrupt nation by at least one study - that of Transparency International.*

- *Conclusion (Isaac's): Mr. Musonge has failed to live up to expectations. Hence the title 'Shouldn't Musonge resign?'*

- *Implication: Resignation is the only thing that is consistent with Musonge's reputation. Isaac does not question Musonge's integrity. Far from it. He presumes that the PM's character is intact, and that it is indeed other forces - other factors if you will - that have derailed his anti-corruption initiative, in which case that character, that integrity, can only be preserved if he resigns.*

There are many contestable points here of course, but the contention by Kate that Isaac ought to call for the resignation of the entire cabinet is not one of them.

Why not?

I am glad you asked. Because his call for the resignation of the PM is predicated by the gentleman's reputation of integrity. He makes no such presumption about the PM's colleagues. In fact it is implied that the PM may not want to be tainted by lesser men by continuing to associate with them. If he cannot reform them, he should at least distance himself from them. That is what a man of integrity would be expected to do.

And this leads to my favorite part - the irony (I am partial to irony because it is manifestation of a form of judgement that never fails, a truth that must peak out from under the piles of obscurantist crapoli with which men seek to hide their unholy intentions). The irony in this situation is that it is Musonge himself who has set the standards by which friend and foe alike can single him out for sanction. That, naturally, is the flip side of the distinction of an approbatory nature that he has enjoyed. By his past deeds - real or staged - he came into government amid high praise, which led to high expectations, which, unfulfilled, leads to high disappointment.

Heaven is the place for the reformed sinner. Hell is the place for the fallen angel.

Steve.

****

On September 30, 1998, Lyombe Eko wrote:

Mola Endeley,

I read with interest, your spirited submissions on the tenure and achievements or lack thereof, of Mola Mafany Musonge, Prime Minister of Cameroon. I must commend you for the independence of mind and intellectual honesty apparent in your piece. I am sure you would have asked the same question if the Prime Minister were Djeukam Tchameni, John Fru Ndi or Joseph Owona, and we found ourselves in such dire straits. Unfortunately, the same cannot be said for the many-headed Camnet market mob which totally ignored the points you raised and quickly wrestled the matter down to the tribal ghetto or rather gutter which many of them inhabit.

I am convinced that your analysis of the tenure of Mola Musonge, who hails from the HFako mountain area like you and I, is devoid of any tribal considerations. If anything, it is nationalistic and shows independence of thought. The problem is that most people on Camnet live in their narrow tribal and/or regional cocoons and therefore cannot believe that you can criticize your own tribe's man, unless of course you have ulterior motives--that is to say, you or someone else in your family aspires to replace Mola Musonge. I would encourage you to treat such trash with the contempt it deserves. Even people who have never been accused of being above "herd and group-think" have a right to "their" collective opinion.

Even though I have been a consistent and caustic critic of the Biya regime and its lamentable failures, I am not inclined to, and do not here call on Mola Musonge to resign. Whether he does a good or bad job is, in my considered opinion, immaterial at this stage. You see, it is not my place to judge someone else's servant. I do not recall that Cameroonians elected Mola Mafany Musonge. If they did, I certainly didn't vote for him. The man is not responsible to the people. He is the errand boy of Paul Biya and he can be fired at Biya's pleasure. We have no say in the matter. Mola Musonge is not the British Prime Minister or even the French Prime Minister. He can of course resign of his own free will but you and I cannot make him resign. You seem to imply that Mola Musonge can save his reputation by leaving the catch 22 no-win situation in which he finds himself. You may be right but resignation at this stage may be personally dangerous for Mola Musonge--ask Garga Haman and Agbor Tabi.

My above statement notwithstanding, calling for Mola Musonge's resignation may be a good academic exercise, a safety valve through which real and imagined grievances against him and by extension, his tribe, can be expressed. However, in the final analysis, all the emotional outpourings and tribalistic vitriol we have witnessed here are as futile as trying to create a river in the desert with tears. The "powers that be" in Cameroon (Paul Biya) couldn't care less.

Resignation may be a good thing in a democratic country. In a corrupt and dictatorial country like Cameroon, it can be downright dangerous. I wouldn't wish that for Mola Musonge who is arguably one of the most competent persons in the Cameroon government.

Have a productive day, Mola.

Lyombe Eko

****

Date: Thu Oct 01 02:07:28 1998
To: CAMNET
From: Isaac Endeley
Subject: **Re: Shouldn't Musonge Resign?**

Oh, Steve and Lyombe:

What would "Planet Camnet" be like without guys like you? I
quiver at the thought! But what took you gentlemen so long to inject
some of the usual common sense into this debate? (Btw, Steve, are
you a reformed sinner or a fallen angel?)

Thanks for the breath of fresh air.

Mola Njoh Endeley.

****

On P. M. Musonge's Tenure

Introduction

In this last installment of the debate between "character" and
"institutions," the focus is on Prime Minister Peter Musonge's
economic record and his government's ability –or the lack thereof–
to improve living conditions for the vast majority of Cameroonians.
Reference is made to a report released a bit earlier that year by the
London-based publisher, the Economist Intelligence Unit (EIU). The
EIU quarterly reports typically contained in-depth analyses of the
economic performance of Cameroon and other countries and were
often relied upon by scholars and investors to gauge the level of
political stability. In this instance my interpretation of the economic
performance and forecasts were clearly at variance with that of my
interlocutor. It was not just a matter of seeing the proverbial glass as

85

half-full or half-empty. It was, to my mind, the difference between reality and "political spin."

Date: Sun, 4 Oct 1998 12:06:23 -0400
Sender: CAMNET
From: Isaac Endeley
Subject: **Re: Musonge's balance sheet two years after...**

Dear Pierre Faa:

Once again, you have proved yourself to be a worthy opponent in a debate. I may not agree with the substance of your analysis, but I admire the civility, clarity, coherence and consistency with which you make your case. Quite sincerely, yours is the kind of reaction I was hoping to elicit from those who argue that Mr. Musonge should stay on as Prime Minister.

Before delving into the nitty-gritty of the debate, let me take a moment to restate my position. I do not question Mr. Musonge's competence and integrity as an individual. My contention is simply that he has failed to live up to the great expectations he raised at the inception of his mandate. He, himself, set the standards by which he is being judged. His failure or inability to effect meaningful change can perhaps be explained by external forces (i.e. he is probably the right man in the right job in the wrong circumstances). However, the longer he lingers on in that portfolio, the harder it will be for him to justify his actions —or inaction— to posterity. That is the context in which I am reiterating my call for him to step aside.

While not wishing to challenge the conclusions of the EIU reports you have cited below, I would like to draw your attention to the fact that these are essentially *macro*-economic analyses. As we all (should) know, the Cameroonian government long ago abdicated its macro-economic management responsibilities to the Bretton Woods institutions. (Mr. Sadou Hayatou, as Minister of Finance, signed the first agreement in 1989 --an achievement for which he was

86

subsequently rewarded with the premiership.) Any success in that domain should therefore be credited to the Structural Adjustment Programmes (SAPs) imposed on us by the World Bank and the IMF. Indeed, as you, yourself, state below, "Macro-economically speaking Cameroon is doing very good." You also refer, quite rightly, to "the sustained work of the government to meet IMF terms." Well, did the government have a choice? Nobody would lend us any more money until we got the IMF's approval. A drowning man will clutch at a straw, as the saying goes. The Enhanced Structural Adjustment Facility (ESAF) agreement signed with the same Washington institutions in August 1997 is merely another nail in our collective coffin.

And what about the government's record at the *micro*-economic level? As if in answer to this question, you make this concession: "One may argue that macro-economic success is yet to trickle down to the man on the street." You bet it is! But shouldn't the government's primary responsibility be to "the man on the street"? Amid all the talk of privatisation (i.e. selling off our companies to the French), what significant improvement has there been in the quality of the average Cameroonian's life? How many Cameroonians who were out of work two years ago can boast of having a job today? How many of our university graduates in the country can find something useful to do with their lives today? To what do you attribute the crime wave sweeping across the country? How do you explain the fact that Yaoundé is termed Africa's filthiest capital? How can one feel comfortable in a sparkling-clean house that is surrounded by mountains of garbage and human waste?

You further state that: "Salaries in the public service have increased substantially (20-30%) even though they are still below their 1987 level." Is that what you call progress? We are worse off today than we were 11 years ago and you think this is worth celebrating? I know Mr. Musonge is no magician, but these are some of the little things I honestly expected him to accomplish during the first few months of his tenure. In my initial posting along this thread, I also alluded to the United Nations Development Programme's 'Human

Development Index' report for 1998 in which Cameroon's declining living standards are clearly chronicled. The Transparency International report on corruption, released a few weeks later, was barely the icing on the cake. Together, they point to a disappointing inability to improve our collective lot.

On the political front, you allege that: "Quietly but efficiently, Musonge has embarked on real political dialogue with the main opposition parties." Where is the evidence? Talks with the SDF lasted barely a few weeks before breaking down irreparably eight months ago. Surely, you are not thinking of Mr. Maigari's UNDP, or Mr. Dakole's MDR, or Mr. Nlend's faction of the UPC! What kind of 'dialogue' can there possibly be when Professor Mendo Ze still dictates which political parties can have access to *Expression Directe* on CRTV? How can you talk of a 'dialogue' when opposition politicians and sympathisers are regularly rounded up and thrown in jail without charge? Yeah, the situation may have been stabilised, but it is the kind of stability that comes from intimidation and harassment. For all we know, it might just be the calm before the storm.

I am quite aware of Mr. Musonge's capabilities, his record and his reputation. Ironically, it is because I hold Mr. Musonge in such high esteem that I would like him to resign. The reason is that he has no real power to take any initiative or to effect any meaningful change. He is a mere "errand boy" to the real powers that be. What bothers me is that he surely knows he can't do much in the current set-up, yet he is staying on. I fear that in the end History may judge him very harshly. It is primarily from this perspective that I call on him to quit now. Twenty-four months is a long enough time for him to assess his own effectiveness --or lack thereof.

Finally, I hate to drag personal or family matters into a public discussion, but if you will allow me a little indiscretion this once, dear Pierre, I would like to conclude on a personal note. Readers who were on this forum in the run-up to the 1997 parliamentary and presidential elections will surely recall this deadly serious quip directed at the Bakweri people: "President Biya has scratched our back [by appointing Mr. Musonge as P.M.], so we should scratch his [by voting en masse for the CPDM] ". This quote, first posted by our fellow Camnetter Monza Dinga (a.k.a Bishop), was attributed to the Paramount Chief of Buea, Chief S.M.L. Endeley. I raise this issue here just to point out that not every person whose last name is Endeley is calling on Mr. Musonge to resign. Contrary to what has been bandied around by some people lacking your finely tuned analytical skills, there is no "family feud" between the Endeleys and the Musonges. I am acquainted with Mr. Musonge and at the personal level I have nothing but admiration for him. At the political level, however, I am disappointed with his performance. My call on him to resign is completely independent of any outside considerations. I value my intellectual freedom very highly.

Once again, I say Mr. Musonge should resign.

Best wishes.

Mola Njoh Endeley.

Chapter IV

On Political Violence

The Right to Bear Arms

Introduction

For some Cameroonians who were beginning to despair about the possibility of achieving a peaceful transfer of power from an autocratic or dictatorial régime to a democratic dispensation, the idea of an armed insurrection appeared quite appealing by the late 1990s. The proponents of this point of view generally argued that in order to eliminate the tyranny of the few over the many, everyone in the country should be allowed to bear arms so that they can protect themselves from oppression or challenge the régime if necessary.

The rejoinder below was in response to a suggestion that "the right to bear arms" should be specifically and explicitly enshrined in the Constitution of Cameroon so that any citizen who desires a firearm can procure it without apprehension. I argue that it is a dangerous proposition to encourage the use of firearms as a means of defending civil and political rights. I point out in particular that although there is some merit in the idea of protecting citizens from armed robbers and common criminals, it would be totally irresponsible for a political party to adopt the threat of an armed conflict as a bargaining chip. For one thing, the Biya régime and its armed forces can muster considerably more firepower than any combination of opposition parties and the régime has proven its willingness to use armed violence to retain power. For another, in the final analysis it is the ordinary citizens who will suffer if armed violence is allowed to break out in Cameroon. .

Date: Fri, 27 Feb 1998 00:21:04 -0500
Sender: CAMNET
From: Isaac Endeley
Subject: **Re: The Right to Bear Arms**

Dear KMF and Akere:

The right of Cameroonians to bear firearms has never been explicitly proscribed by law, and there is no reason why it should be explicitly prescribed either. When I was growing up along the slopes of Mount Fako, many people, including several close relatives of mine, who earned a living out of hunting in the surrounding forests, owned duly registered firearms. The weapons ranged from simple revolvers to fairly sophisticated semi-automatic rifles. To the best of my recollection, all they needed to do (in the 1960s and 1970s) was to obtain a security clearance (or permit) from the police and take it to the gun shop. In those days a certain Chief Arrey in Limbe ran one of the best-known gun shops around.

The main set-back for most would-be gun owners at the time was the prohibitive cost of the firearms and the attendant ammunition, since a regular shotgun was priced in the hundreds of thousands of francs CFA, and a double-barreled weapon cost even more. Nonetheless, people managed to buy them, and some of the more successful hunters even had gun collections. The prerequisites for the permit may have been modified in recent years, but the last time I was in my village I still saw many a hunter with a gun.

However, I do not think it has ever occurred to these people to use their firearms for political purposes. I still remember how in days of yore Ahidjo's *Gendarmes* used to burst into my village in the wee hours of the morning to round up those suspected of tax evasion (the infamous "*callé-callé*"), but I don't recall a single incident in which the villagers put up an armed resistance. This could perhaps be explained by the overwhelming firepower of the forces of law and order, or maybe by the sheer futility of such an exercise. Whatever the case, I think it is dangerous to transform the political process into an armed

92

struggle. I find it totally irresponsible for anyone to suggest that opposition parties wishing to be taken seriously by the government should stockpile firearms and use them as bargaining chips!

That said, I hasten to point out that I see some merit in the drive to protect citizens from armed robbers and other criminals. Recent reports from Cameroon would seem to suggest that the security situation has deteriorated beyond recognition and that the police force is totally incapable of doing its job. Indeed, in some instances police officers have been accused of being willing accomplices to the criminal gangs. Growing numbers of law-abiding citizens are now resorting to unorthodox means to protect their lives and property. It has become, quite literally, a matter of life and death in some parts of the country.

Some big questions remain, though. For instance, where do we draw the line between the political and the security arenas? How can we ensure that a firearm acquired for security purposes will not be used to further other ends? Is there a way of guaranteeing the people's protection without promoting the proliferation of firearms? Can our national police force be rehabilitated?

The hiring of private security firms is obviously one solution that appears to be working in many parts of Africa today, but can the average Cameroonian afford to pay for such services? I don't claim to have the answer to any of these questions, but I hope the search continues and I pray that we can find a solution before things get any worse.

Peace to all,

Mola Njoh Endeley.

****

Captain Guérandi Mbara

Introduction

Captain Guérandi Mbara is a former officer of the Cameroon Armed Forces. He hails from the northern part of the country and is believed to have been associated with the failed attempt by military officers to overthrow the Biya régime in April 1984. Following the failure of the *putsch*, Captain Mbara fled Cameroon and was believed to have sought refuge in Burkina Faso or elsewhere in West Africa.

During the late 1990s Captain Mbara became an infrequent participant in the Camnet debates. His contributions were often in the form of lengthy monologues castigating the Biya Government and reminiscing about the good old days of the Ahidjo dictatorship. In the period from May 1997 to January 1998, he published on Camnet a series of six extensive "bulletins" essentially calling on members of the Cameroon Armed Forces to unite, rise up and overthrow the government. He suggested that if the military did not heed his call to topple the Biya régime, a bloody civil war was likely to break out in the country.

In my response reproduced here, I attempt to show that for the average Cameroonian –excluding Northerners like Captain Mbara– life under the Ahidjo régime was not a bed of roses. I point out that both President Ahidjo and his successor, President Biya, have been brutal dictators who have used the same methods –including tribalism, cronyism and nepotism– to stay in power. I argue that the main difference between the two régimes is the global politico-economic context in which the country finds itself. (My e-mail to Captain Mbara is in French but I provide an English translation in a footnote.)

"G. M." ... a écrit:

CAMEROUN

CRIMINALITE GOUVERNANTE, FERMENT D'UNE
GUERRE CIVILE *L'urgence d'une prévention*

[...]

*Patriotes des Forces Armées, quelle défense pourrions-nous assurer sans le
soutien et l'appui des populations? Quand allons-nous enfin créer les conditions
véritables de réconciliation avec le Peuple camerounais?*

Le 20 mai 1997

Le Capitaine GUERANDI MBARA[7]

Date: Mon, 12 Jan 1998 19:02:19 -0500
Sender: CAMNET
From: Isaac Endeley
Subject: **Re: MEMORANDUM - Bulletin 6 de 6 -**
FINALE

Cher Capitaine Guérandi Mbara,

Bonne année à vous et merci de nous avoir fait part de vos réflexions sur la crise de leadership que connait depuis longtemps notre chère patrie. Vous faites dans vos six bulletins un excellent travail de dépistage et vous pointez du doigt toutes les faiblesses du régime actuel. On ne saurait vous en remercier suffisamment.

Mais, ma foi, que vous avez la mémoire courte ! Vous semblez donner l'impression que les problèmes du Cameroun n'ont commencé qu'en 1982 avec l'accession de M. Paul Biya à la magistrature suprême. A vous lire, un observateur non-averti pourrait en arriver à la conclusion que pendant le règne du dictateur Ahmadou Ahidjo les Camerounais vivaient dans un paradis africain. Ca l'était probablement pour vous, en tant que ressortissant de la région d'Ahidjo et en votre qualité d'officier de l'Armée camerounaise. Mais vous étiez quand-même en mesure de constater la misère de la plupart de vos compatriotes. Vous qui cherchez aujourd'hui à nous donner des leçons sur la démocratie, où étiez-vous lorsque les gorilles d'Ahidjo réprimaient tous ceux qui osaient prononcer un discours différent de celui du régime? Vous êtes allé jusqu'à qualifier de <<soulèvement patriotique>> le putsch manqué d'avril 1984. Soulèvement patriotique mon œil ! Pourquoi ces militaires ne se sont-ils pas soulevés pour démontrer leur patriotisme à l'égard des villageois qu'ils étaient souvent appelés à éliminer pour le compte du régime d'Ahidjo?

Entre la dictature d'Ahidjo et celle de Biya, il n'y a qu'une seule différence fondamentale: celle de la conjoncture. La structure de l'État est demeurée essentiellement la même; les deux leaders ont employé les mêmes moyens pour se maintenir au pouvoir: le

96

tribalisme, le régionalisme et le népotisme à l'égard de leurs proches; la fraude, la répression et la terreur à l'endroit des populations. L'un s'est révélé tout aussi corrompu et tout aussi assoiffé de pouvoir que l'autre. L'un et l'autre, ainsi que leurs acolytes, ont pillé les caisses de l'État pour s'enrichir et faire gonfler leurs comptes dans les banques suisses alors que les citoyens souffrent et meurent de pauvreté au pays. La mauvaise gestion de la chose publique n'est pas une nouveauté non plus. Si de nombreux Camerounais se disent aujourd'hui nostalgiques de la période d'Ahidjo, ce n'est point parce que le feu dictateur était d'un pouce plus bénin que son fourbe de successeur. C'est notamment parce que la conjoncture de l'époque lui permettait de satisfaire à la plupart des besoins économiques des Camerounais, et ce malgré les fraudes orchestrées par certains barons du régime. De plus, le contexte politique international lui assurait le soutien des pays occidentaux, surtout la France.

Par contre, depuis quelques années la conjoncture s'est profondément modifiée avec la chute des prix de nos produits d'exportation sur le marché mondial. En outre, dans le nouvel ordre mondial, les fameuses conditionnalités des pays occidentaux bailleurs de fonds et des institutions financières internationales sont désormais monnaie courante. Ceci a eu pour conséquence de baisser les revenus de l'État et donc de diminuer sa capacité de tout maitriser. Vous connaissez sans doute la suite.

On remarque en passant que vous terminez votre long exposé en lançant un appel aux <<Patriotes des Forces Armées>> pour qu'ils s'allient avec vous. Comme justification, vous évoquez le spectre d'une guerre civile. On suppose alors qu'une telle alliance aurait pour but de monter un coup d'État militaire au Cameroun.

De prime abord, vous devriez noter qu'à travers l'histoire de l'humanité toute entière, les militaires n'ont jamais fait de bons politiciens. Il suffit de jeter un coup d'œil sur les événements qui se sont succédés en Afrique contemporaine depuis les indépendances pour se rendre compte de l'incapacité des militaires à gérer un pays. Que ce soit au Nigeria, au Ghana, au Libéria, au Benin ou encore au Burkina Faso, les leaders militaires se sont souvent révélés plus corrompus et plus meurtriers que les régimes civils qu'ils prétendaient remplacer. En deuxième lieu, la complexité de la nation camerounaise rendrait très couteuse et très sanglante toute tentative d'y monter un coup d'État. C'est assez décevant que vous n'ayez pas appris cette leçon à la suite du putsch manqué d'avril 1984 !

Si vous cherchez une véritable réconciliation nationale au Cameroun, vous feriez mieux de poursuivre la voie du dialogue. C'est déjà un bon début d'avoir entrepris la rédaction de votre mémorandum et de l'avoir fait parvenir à vos compatriotes, et il faut vous en féliciter. Mais puisque vous semblez nourrir une grande ambition politique, vous devriez faire davantage. Vous auriez dû vous associer avec un parti politique, par exemple. Le Chef de l'État actuel n'a-t-il pas gracié tous les putschistes de 1984 ? En tout cas, on espère que la paix l'emportera sur la guerre.

Permettez-moi de m'arrêter ici pour le moment, cher Capitaine, tout en espérant reprendre bientôt le dialogue avec vous. Veuillez agréer l'expression de mes sentiments les meilleurs.[8] *Isaac Njoh Endeley.*

---

[8] Dear Captain Guérandi Mbara :

Happy New Year to you and thank you for informing us of your thoughts on the leadership crisis from which our country has been suffering for a long time. In your six bulletins, you have performed an excellent analysis and you have clearly identified the main weaknesses of the current régime. I cannot thank you enough for this.

But, goodness gracious, what a short memory you seem to have! You give the impression that Cameroon's problems only started in 1982 with Mr. Paul Biya's elevation to the highest office in the land. An uninformed reader of your writings would think that during the reign of the dictator Ahmadou Ahidjo Cameroonians were living in an African paradise. It was probably an African paradise for you since you are from the same region as Ahidjo and since you were an officer of the Cameroon Army. Nonetheless, you must have noticed that the majority of your compatriots lived in misery. You who are now trying to teach us about democracy, where were you when Ahidjo's henchmen were brutalizing those who dared to express views different from the régime's? You even went as far as describing the failed *coup d'Etat* of April 1984 as a "popular uprising." Popular uprising, my little finger! Why didn't those soldiers rise up to show their patriotism in defence of the villagers they were often called upon to eliminate on behalf of the Ahidjo régime?

There is only one real difference between the Ahidjo and Biya dictatorships, and that relates to the general economic circumstances. The structure of the State has remained essentially the same; both leaders have used the same methods to maintain themselves in power, namely tribalism, regionalism and nepotism in relation to those close to them, and fraud, repression and terror towards the general population. The one is just as corrupt and power-hungry as the other. Both of them, as well as their acolytes, have pillaged the State coffers to enrich themselves and stuff their Swiss bank accounts while their citizens suffer and die of poverty at home. The poor management of public affairs is not new either. Although many Cameroonians today are nostalgic about the Ahidjo era, it is not because the late dictator was any more benevolent than his guileful successor. It is mostly because the economic circumstances of that era allowed him to satisfy most of the economic demands of Cameroonians, and this was in spite of the fraud orchestrated by some of the régime's stalwarts. Moreover, due to the international political climate, Ahidjo had the full backing of Western countries, particularly France.

Conversely, for some years now the economic circumstances have changed drastically with the fall in the prices of our export products on the world market. In addition, in the New World Order the famous conditions imposed by Western donor nations and the international financial institutions have become commonplace. As a consequence the State's revenues, as well as its ability to control everything, have been reduced. You are doubtless familiar with the rest of the story.

I also note that you end your long exposé by calling on the "Patriots of the Armed Forces" to form an alliance with you. As a justification, you refer to a looming civil war. It thus appears that the goal of your proposed alliance is to stage a military *coup d'Etat* in Cameroon.

First of all, you should realise that throughout human history soldiers have never been good politicians. Just take a look at successive events in contemporary Africa since the years of independence and you will see that the military are incapable of running a country. Whether it is in Nigeria, Ghana, Liberia, Benin or

****

The Kidnapping!

Introduction

In the run-up to the October 1997 presidential elections in Cameroon, which the SDF and other leading opposition parties had decided to boycott, a number of obscure candidates opted to enter the race. One such candidate was Mr. Christopher Nsahlai, an Anglophone politician from the North-West Province. Approximately one month before the election, Mr. Nsahlai's wife was allegedly abducted by unknown persons and held incommunicado for about a week. It was believed that the abduction had taken place in the same general area where the Government's *Gendarmerie* facilities had come under armed attack in March 1997.

Then, on 19 September 1997, it was announced on Camnet that Mrs. Nsahlai had been released by her captors, who did not clearly identify themselves or their cause and did not formulate any specific

---

Burkina Faso, the military leaders have turned out to be even more corrupt and murderous than the civilian régimes they purported to replace. Secondly, due to the complexity of the Cameroonian nation, any attempt to stage a *coup d'Etat* there will prove very costly and bloody. It is quite disappointing to note that you did not learn this lesson in the aftermath of the failed *putsch* of April 1984!

If you want real national reconciliation in Cameroon, you would do well to pursue the path of dialogue. You have already made a good start by drafting your memorandum and circulating it among your compatriots, and I congratulate you for that. However, since you appear to have greater political ambitions, you should do more. For instance, you should have joined a political party. Hasn't the current Head of State pardoned all those involved in the 1984 *putsch*? In any event, I hope peace will triumph over war.

Let me stop here for now, dear Captain, but I hope to pursue this dialogue with you soon. Please accept my best regards.

demands. Consequently, there was considerable speculation on Camnet as to who the abductors were and what their motives might have been.

Given the prevailing political context in Cameroon, many Camnet contributors concluded that President Paul Biya and his governing CPDM party were behind the abduction of Mrs. Nsahlai as a means of pressuring her husband into withdrawing from the race. In the e-mail below, I argue that spousal abduction does not appear to fit in with Mr. Biya's *modus operandi*. Besides, if such were his intent, he would surely have gone for a much less obscure target. Rather, I posit that Anglophone separatists, with whom Mr. Nsahlai had flirted in the past, were the most likely culprits.

On September 19, 1997, Acha Leke wrote:

heard she was found ALIVE in the jungles 100 miles from Bamenda....have no further details...

......acha.

Date: Sun, 21 Sep 1997 20:45:48 -0400
Sender: CAMNET
From: Isaac Endeley
Subject: **The Kidnapping!**

Hi, Acha:

I'm relieved to learn that Mrs. Nsahlai's ordeal is finally over. But unlike some on this forum, I don't think Mr. Biya or his government had anything to do with the kidnapping. I'm far from believing that Mr. Nsahlai's bid for the presidency posed a credible threat to Mr. Biya's chances of retaining power. On the contrary, given that the current electoral law provides for only one round of voting, it would be in the incumbent's best interest to have as many minor opponents

101

as possible in the presidential contest. Besides, with Mr. Biya's three biggest challengers (Messrs Ndi, Maigari and Njoya) officially out of the race, and with the outcome pretty much a foregone conclusion, any additional contestant would only serve to give the process an extra dose of legitimacy. Furthermore, if spousal abduction were Mr. Biya's style, he would surely have gone for a less obscure and more menacing target.

What I do suspect, however, is that ghosts and other shady characters from Mr. Nsahlai's checkered political past have begun resurfacing to haunt him. To my mind, the key to the puzzle is to be found in his well-documented flirtation with the Anglophone separatist movement. I suspect that the responsibility for the abduction lies with some of the more radical elements in the youth wing of that movement. (Yes indeed, the same ones who are being "credited" with undertaking the deadly attacks on Gendarmerie facilities last Easter!) They may have seen Mr. Nsahlai's bid for national office as a betrayal of their narrow parochial aspirations. They might also have seen his candidature as a tacit legitimization of the Biya regime, which they mortally despise. The place and circumstances in which Mrs. Nsahlai was kidnapped and released, as well as the abductors' demands, seem to lead to this conclusion. But I may be wrong ...

Ciao,

Mola Njoh Endeley.

****

Legal Defense Fund

Introduction

In the late 1990s some Cameroonians residing in the United States established a charitable organisation known as the Cryer

Foundation that sought, among other things, to promote the welfare of Cameroonians. In May 1998, the Cryer Foundation launched a drive on Camnet to collect funds for the legal representation of the men accused of conducting the armed attack on *Gendarmerie* facilities in the North-West Province of Cameroon in March 1997. The Cryer Foundation's initial argument was that it was unjustified for the men to be held for more than two years without trial and without the means to defend themselves. The Foundation urged members of the Camnet community to contribute generously to a legal defense fund to represent the accused men.

Some Camnetters questioned the real motives behind the Cryer Foundation's fund-raising drive; others dismissed the Foundation outright, arguing that the accused men had committed unjustifiable acts of political violence and should not be given succour. At the same time a few contributors, including myself, argued for a balanced approach, urging the Cryer Foundation, as a neutral and non-partisan organisation, to consider mobilising financial and legal support not only for the men accused of carrying out the acts of violence, but also for their alleged victims, those who became widowed and orphaned as s result of those acts.

The brief exchanges reproduced here represent a query by one Camnetter seeking an explanation, followed by an explanation from a representative of the Foundation, and finally my challenge to the Cryer Foundation to adopt a more balanced approach.

On May 17, 1999, Ndzie Germain-Blaise wrote:

Salut Atem Ebini!

Voici deux ans que des Camerounais sont retenus pour enquête. Ceci est inadmissible. C'est vrai. Mais j'aimerais savoir si pendant tout ce temps la CRYER FOUNDATION aurait aussi un moment pensé à lancer un appel pour rassembler des fonds pour ces femmes et enfants qui ont perdu leurs papas dans cet acte que les accusés d'aujourd'hui sont supposés avoir commis. En tant que association non partisane je pense qu'il serait nécessaire de ne pas seulement suivre certaines actions (rassembler des fonds maintenant pour la défense). Ne devenez pas les défenseurs d'un groupe. C'est ainsi qu'on jugera votre non-alignement et votre humanisme.

Bonne journée.[9]
ndzie.

On May 17, 1999, Christmas Atem Ebini wrote:

Mr. Ndzie:

The CRYER Foundation is a small and new organization. We are committed to what we do and we have great faith that the future would be bright for the foundation and the people and nation it was created to serve.

Please do be patient with our present limitations and give us time.

Ebini Atem Christmas.

---

[9] Hi, Atem Ebini!

It has now been two years since some Cameroonians were detained for investigations. It is true that this is unacceptable. However, I would like to know if during the same period the CRYER FOUNDATION has considered launching an appeal for funds to assist the wives and children who lost their husbands and fathers as a result of those acts that the detained men are accused of committing. As a non-partisan association, the CRYER FOUNDATION should not follow only one line of action (that of collecting funds now for the legal defense). Do not become the defenders of one group only. That is how your non-alignment and your humanism will be judged.

Have a nice day.

Date: Tue, 18 May 1999 09:10:33 +0200
Sender: CAMNET
From: Isaac Endeley
Subject: **Re: The Cryer Foundation and the Legal Defense Fund**

Hello, Christmas:

I believe Germain-Blaise raises a valid and legitimate concern and it should not be dismissed lightly on the grounds that the Cryer Foundation is a nascent organisation. As a *bona fide* and non-partisan entity, the Foundation should not be seen to be favouring one side over the other(s).

Whatever one may think of the people directly involved in the March 1997 incident, the truth remains that when those terrorist attacks were orchestrated, at least ten people were killed. Those ten people had families, which probably include some orphans and widows today. Shouldn't the Cryer Foundation be making an equally commendable effort to provide these forgotten victims with some form of relief?

As a matter of fact, given the meagre resources currently available to the Foundation, wouldn't it be easier and more productive to focus on this smaller task that is easier to accomplish, rather than tackle the herculean feat of setting up a legal defense fund? At the very least, in a bid to maintain a semblance of neutrality, the Cryer Foundation should consider undertaking both actions simultaneously. That way it can forestall any accusations of partisanship.

What do you think?

Warmest regards.

Mola Njoh Endeley.

****

Testimony of Ange Tekam (Thatcher)

Introduction

The story of Ms. Guiadem Ange Tekam, nicknamed "Margaret Thatcher", received considerable attention from Camnetters from 1997 to 1999. Apparently, during the World Conference on Women, that took place in Beijing, China from 4 to 15 September 1995, a report was presented to the delegates detailing acts of brutality committed by the Cameroon Government against Ms. Tekam on account of her political views. The rather long and moving report was subsequently posted on Camnet in September 1997 and afforded participants the opportunity to analyze it and formulate their own views.

The debate that ensued on Camnet centred on the use of violence to further political ends. In particular, it focused on the widespread abuse of human rights in Cameroon and the Government's well-known propensity to use the forces of law and order as a tool for violently suppressing political dissent.

The full report is omitted here but the e-mail below summarises my initial reactions upon reading the report. I then respond to a series of questions posed by a follow-Camnetter who pushed me to elaborate on my proposals. Finally, when Ms. Tekam herself joined Camnet in May 1999, I was one of the first to welcome her. Unfortunately, she never responded either directly or indirectly to any of the questions I posed to her.

Date: Fri, 5 Sep 1997 19:58:01 -0400
Sender: Discussion on Cameroon's Topics
From: Nicoline Ambe
Subject: **Testimony of Ange Tekam (Thatcher)**

Netters,

I'd like to share with you the testimony of Guiadem Ange Tekam (Fondly known as Margaret Thatcher), a former student of the University of Yaoundé. Her testimony was given before the Beijing Tribunal on Accountability for Human Rights in Beijing, China. For those who do not know "Thatcher", she was a female student activist who dedicated most of her time to the activities of "la conférence", a former pro-democracy student body of the University of Yaoundé.

STATE SPONSORED PERSECUTION OF GENDER BASED VIOLENCE: THE STORY OF CAMEROON STUDENT ACTIVIST GUIADEM ANGE TEKAM.
[...]

Date: Sun, 7 Sep 1997 15:56:29 -0400
Sender: CAMNET
From: Isaac Endeley
Subject: **Re: Testimony of Ange Tekam (Thatcher)**

Dear Nicoline:

Thank you very much for sharing with us the story of Guiadem Ange Tekam (a.k.a. Margaret Thatcher). Her testimony brings to light yet another instance of the unrivalled brutality of our so-called forces of law and order in Cameroon. I deplore the inhuman treatment to which she was subjected and I hope no effort will be spared to prosecute the individuals responsible for those actions. But beyond that, I hope we can all continue to work to eliminate the kinds of institutions and cultural practices that make it possible for some human beings to do such cruel deeds to others. Ms. Tekam's story is very moving, but, unfortunately for Cameroon, it is not unique. There are many other individuals suffering a similar fate at the hands of our *Gendarmes* on a daily basis. (The story of Eric Kwati's family last May comes to mind most readily.) Drastic action needs to be taken to restore basic human rights in Cameroon, and I'm sure this is something on which we can all agree, regardless of our ethnic, political, religious, linguistic or other differences. A good first step would be to sensitize the public, both national and international, and I'm pleased to observe that this is already being done in Ms. Tekam's case. But the method (and not the substance) raises a couple of questions.

1) Given that her testimony was presented to "The Beijing Tribunal on Accountability for Women's Human Rights," I can't help but wonder: Was she persecuted for being a political activist, a student leader, a newspaper editor, and a strident opponent of the regime (i.e. regardless of gender), or was she persecuted merely for being a woman?

2) Isn't it something of an oxymoron to raise human rights concerns in Beijing?

Whatever the case, I hope the culprits can be brought to justice swiftly. Meanwhile, let us all continue to examine the various ways in which we can contribute towards improving the human rights situation in Cameroon.

Thanks again and best regards,

Mola Njoh Endeley.

Date: Mon, 8 Sep 1997 22:40:21 -0400
Sender: CAMNET
From: Isaac Endeley
Subject: **Re: Testimony of Ange Tekam (Thatcher)**

Hello, Pa Atekwana:

As always, it was quite a pleasure to read from you. I think I understand the points you've raised so far in this discussion, but permit me to respond to the specific questions you posed in reaction to my previous contribution.

You asked:

Under the present situation in Cameroon who is the one to ensure that "no effort will be spared to prosecute the individuals responsible for those actions?"

I take this to imply that, given the current state of affairs, we cannot rely on the competent authorities to perform this basic judiciary function, and I subscribe to this assessment. Fortunately, in Ms. Tekam's Testimony forwarded to us by Nicoline Ambe, she alludes to the involvement of the Public Prosecutor, a journalist, "a woman jurist and the Association for the Struggle Against Violence Against Women". These are the people to whom I was referring.

You further wrote:

I am of the opinion that we should talk of Beijing's violations of human rights with caution. I would also believe that Ms. Tekam presented this not to the Beijing Government but at or as a prolongation of the holding in Beijing of the International Conference on the Rights of the Woman.

In the final analysis, perhaps an evaluation of China's performance on human rights issues is really a matter of personal opinion. I was merely querying the expediency of raising such

109

concerns in Beijing, considering that the Chinese have virtually no clout or credibility in these matters. Besides, the evidence presented in Ms. Tekam's own Testimony would seem to indicate that she was tortured for being an opponent of the regime rather than simply because she is female. Thus there are two reasons why the choice of Beijing appears questionable. However, I do not wish to downplay the traumatic effects of her experiences and I still hope people I mentioned above can prosecute the culprits swiftly.

You added:

And besides, even if she did them, a humane army will treat women differently from men under similar conditions.

Well, I don't know about that, Pa Atekwana. I believe a truly humane law-enforcement agency should treat all human beings in an equally humane manner, regardless of gender.

Finally, you suggested:

While thanking all compatriots for debating topics of interest to our fatherland, I would like that at the "end" of every topic we come up with a summary of concrete actions to alleviate the situation. That is what to do, when to do it, who to do it, with what to do it etc.

I think this is a very good idea. Perhaps we should agree that whoever initiates a discussion on any given subject should be responsible for drawing up a summary of that discussion, including all the proposals advanced. I wonder what others think.

Bye for now and all the best,

Mola Njoh Endeley.

Date: Sat, 8 May 1999 21:32:26 +0200
Sender: CAMNET
From: Isaac Endeley
Subject: **Re: Testimony of Ange Tekam (Thatcher)**

Dear Guiadem Ange Tekam:

I'd like to take this opportunity to formally welcome you to
Camnet. Obviously, your reputation precedes you. Thanks to
Nicoline Ambe, we had the opportunity to learn of your traumatic
experiences some 19 months ago. After reading your testimony in
September 1997, a number of us were deeply moved. I recall in
particular that Pa Joe Atekwana and I then had an interesting
discussion about the issue of human rights in Cameroon.

At that time, I had raised a couple of general questions addressed
to Nicoline. However, since you are now on the forum yourself, I
would be grateful if you could find the time to answer them for me.
Please find appended below[10] an unedited copy of my initial reaction
upon reading your testimony in September 1997.

Once again, welcome to Camnet.

Warmest regards,

Mola Njoh Endeley.

---

[10] There is no need to reproduce the e-mail from September 1997 here since
the reader will already have seen it in the pages immediately preceding this one.

111

Chapter V

On Freedom of Expression in Cameroon

On Freedom of Expression in Cameroon

Introduction

By the late 1990s, even as the use of the Internet as a means of communication became more widespread alongside the proliferation of media outlets, the Cameroon Government still appeared intent on maintaining a deathly grip on the dissemination of information about the country. Few incidents could possibly have illustrated this desire for censorship and control more vividly than the disproportionately harsh penalty meted out to veteran journalist Pius Njawé who, in December 1997, published an article in which he speculated that President Biya may have suffered a mild heart attack while watching a football match.

A number of Cameroonians attempted to show their disapproval for the strict censorship by writing copiously, often insultingly, on Camnet and elsewhere. In late 1997, one intrepid Camnetter who had the technical savvy, and who managed to remain anonymous, set up a rather rudimentary web site where he used political parody and satire to ridicule the Biya régime. He labeled the website "Paul Biya's Sexy Home Page" and posted on it not only the written word but also cartoons, caricatures and doctored images of the President and his acolytes.

In February 1998, at a time when the President's latest European vacation was in the news, I was struck by the observation that the number of visitors to "Paul Biya's Sexy Home Page" had risen to more than six million! My e-mail below, in the form or a parody, arrived at the inescapable conclusion that the Cameroonian people did not trust the official Government rhetoric and were in dire need of alternative sources of information. It also confirmed the rise of the Internet as the primary medium by which the Government's monopoly on the control of information would be challenged.

Finally, I have taken the liberty of reproducing another Camnetter's independent assessment of the website in question, as well as the anonymous website creator's statement of his motivations for establishing "Paul Biya's Sexy Home Page."

Date: Sun, 1 Feb 1998 18:06:06 -0500
Sender: CAMNET
From: Isaac Endeley
Subject: **Re: Paul Biya's Sexy Home Page**

Hi, folks:

With the latest shenanigans of U.S. Chief of State "Bubba" Clinton making the headlines around the globe and on Camnet, I thought this might be a good time to see how our very own King of the Jungle, His Majesty Biya bi Mvondo of Mvomeka'a, fares by comparison. But such a delicate analysis as this one is rendered all the more complicated by the contradictory claims made about the "lion man's" heart condition and sexual prowess.

On the one hand, Franck Essomba and Pius Njawé (*Le Messager,* December 22, 1997) allege that Biya is suffering from a debilitating heart ailment which makes him unable to sit through a simple football match. On the other, Thierry Ngoufan (Camnet, January 26, 1998) intimates that traces of Biya's current private visit to Europe can be found at downtown brothels in European capitals. So how can a man with a failing heart be cavorting and frolicking with those hard-hitting, leather-clad, European hookers? That is the question I set out to answer on behalf of all Camnetters and most Cameroonians.

114

For starters, I decided to go directly to the source or, if you prefer, to get it straight from the horse's mouth. I visited (or, rather, revisited) Paul Biya's Sexy Home Page at:

http://www.geocities.com/CapitolHill/Lobby/6895/

Well, there you have it. Live. In glorious technicolor. Sounds like Thierry is right. Which means Njawé must have been wrong. That explains his arrest and incarceration. Two years in prison. For suggesting that King Midas has lost his golden touch. Think about it. Modern-day monarchs mostly thrive on mystique. The palace couldn't afford to have this myth debunked. So they threw Njawé in the slammer. That should shut others up. Meanwhile, His Majesty returns to the brothel. Or is it really to a hospital? Can he have his cake and eat it, too? Ask for a medical report. Before letting him into the brothel. Then again, maybe not. Let the hookers do him in.

One thing I found totally flabbergasting about Biya's Sexy Home Page is the sheer volume of traffic it seems to have attracted over the months. When I first visited it in October 1997, I made a note of the fact that I was visitor # 1,276. Today, February 1st, 1998, I became # 6,172,192!

So who are those six million prurient visitors? Judging by the interest in the Clinton-Lewinsky saga, I imagine Camnetters are not averse to a little titillation. But I strongly suspect that someone at Etoudi palace has bought a computer and is using Intelcam's facilities to surf the 'net late at night. No wonder some are having heart problems.

Nkosi sikelel' i Afrika ![11]

Mola Njoh Endeley.

---

[11] Zulu for "God bless Africa!"

P.S.: Take a moment to re-read these words of wisdom below.

Lyombe Eko wrote:

Dear anonymous friend,

I must confess that I consulted the so-called Paul Biya homepage. I found it vulgar, indecent, and totally tasteless. However, as long as you use the internet, you have a right to express yourself in any manner you see fit. While the caricature of Paul Biya cannot be said to have much literary or artistic value, it has some redeeming value--it is more political or rather politically motivated than sexually motivated.

It occurs to me that when all is said and done, and when the dust settles on this controversy--as it surely must--the issue goes beyond morality and the invasion of Paul Biya's privacy. The issue at hand is power and control. While I would not resort to such tactics to score political points, it seems to me that the homepage is a symbolic wake-up call to those who believe in the absolute, centralized government control of information. Information is power and anyone who has half a brain knows that Paul Biya has led a government which believes in the absolute control of information. Indeed, the global communication revolution is by-passing Cameroon because of the government's absolute control of all sources of information. The internet puts paid to that. It is true that the number of Cameroonians with access to the internet is less than the number of nuts in a 100 francs CFA cup of groundnuts but with technology, that will soon be a thing of the past.

Paul Biya has stated his intention to govern Cameroon for the next 14 years--and he might just do that if the good Lord spares him. The web page in question is an indication of things that might lie ahead for him, as well as for Cameroon, as a result of advancing technology. For once, the government cannot censor, seize or ban information about the head of state. That is a very symbolic situation that should give us food for thought.

Remember that last year in France, the courts banned a book by Dr. Gubler, Mitterand's former personal physician, about Francois Mitterand's deception of the French people with regard to his 14-year struggle with cancer, his mistress and his illegitimate daughter, Mazarine. The banned book was immediately put on

116

the internet and was around the world in no time. In the United States, volunteers quickly translated it into English and put it on several servers and webpages.

Whether we like it or not, we have to learn to live with vulgar things like the Paul Biya homepage. That is the price we all have to pay for strict, government information control.

Regards,
LE

****

On October 28, 1997, "Paul BiyaGai" wrote:

Hi Mr Eko,

Thanks for your mail. It might seem extremely vain of me, but my main aim of coming up with that ridiculous caricature of a web page had nothing to do with the man's sexuality. As you so eloquently point out in your mail, it's a question of control - of pointing out to Mr Biya and his ilk that there are certain things which are absolutely beyond their control. Journalists are being arrested everyday in Cameroon because they dare to tell even a half-truth about Biya. It is not a Beti thing or whatever - the man's government has the likes of Kontchou (whose contention is that a good player - presumably like himself - never lacks a team), or that Musonge guy, and Achu before him.

I am currently assembling what I loosely term 'content' for a Biya domain I'm in the process of registering, so if anyone has anything they want the world to know about Biya and his cronies, please do send it off to me.

Thanks

****

Pius Njawé Released from Prison

Introduction

It will be recalled that during the finals of the Cameroon Football Cup in December 1997, President Biya had to leave the stadium before the end of the match, prompting a lot of speculation at home and on Camnet about the cause of his premature departure. In an article published in *Le Messager* newspaper on 22 December 1997, journalist Pius Njawé suggested that the President may have suffered a heart attack during the match. Njawé was subsequently charged with defamation, arrested, tried and sentenced to a lengthy jail term.

In October 1998 it was reported on Camnet that President Biya, in his magnanimity, had ordered the release of Pius Njawé. The author of the news report attempted to portray the President as a victim, triggering a rather sarcastic response from me.

On October 10, 1998, Olongo Zana wrote:

Compatriotes,

Notre Président vient de prouver une fois de plus sa dimension d'homme d'état magnanime à l'écoute des aspirations de son peuple et respectueux des institutions de notre pays.

Depuis vendredi Pius Njawé, qui avait été incarcéré pour diffamation est un homme libre sur décret de notre Président, la victime de sa diffamation.

Bon week end à tous[12]. Zoloni

Date: Sun, 11 Oct 1998 12:38:04 -0400

---

[12] Compatriots:

Our President has just proved once again that he is a magnanimous statesman who listens to his people's aspirations and respects our country's institutions.

Since last Friday Pius Njawé, who had been imprisoned for defamation, is a free man thanks to a decree signed by our President, the victim of the defamation.

Have a good weekend, everyone.

118

Sender: CAMNET
From: Isaac Endeley
Subject: **Re: Président Paul Biya, homme magnanime!**

Salut, Compatriote Zoloni !

Oui, chantons et dansons ! Sa Majesté Biya bi Mvondo est vraiment le dictateur le plus "magnanime" au monde. Quel autre "homme d'état" aurait pu décréter la libération d'un journaliste incarcéré pour avoir simplement exercé son métier ? Quelle autre "victime" de "diffamation" aurait eu la sagesse d'écouter les voix qui s'élevaient de part et d'autre pour demander que la justice soit faite ? Y a-t-il sur cette planète un autre "Président" qui soit tant "à l'écoute des aspirations de son peuple" ? Que non ! Le monde n'a jamais connu une telle "magnanimité". Surtout lorsqu'on se rend compte du fait que M. Njawé avait déjà purgé la plus grande partie de sa peine et qu'il ne lui restait que moins de trois mois à passer en prison.

D'autres leaders soupçonnés d'avoir subi un malaise cardiaque auraient peut-être cherché à démontrer, dossier médical à l'appui, qu'ils étaient en bonne santé malgré les apparences. Mais pas notre cher Po Mbia, qui est quand-même "respectueux des institutions de notre pays". L'Histoire retiendra sans doute cet aspect de la "démocratie avancée" à la camerounaise ainsi que cette "dimension d'homme d'état magnanime à l'écoute des aspirations de son peuple".

Vive Po Mbia ![13]

---

[13] Hi, Compatriot Zoloni:

Yes, let us sing and dance! His Majesty Biya bi Mvondo is truly the most "magnanimous" dictator in the world. Which other "statesman" would have decreed the freeing of a journalist who was incarcerated simply for doing his job? Which other "victim" of "defamation" could have had the wisdom to listen to all the voices that were being raised from all quarters to demand that justice should be done? Is there any other "President" in this world who "listens to his people's aspirations" so keenly? No! The world has never before seen such "magnanimity."

****

Re: Cameroon News!

Introduction

In September 1998, I posted on Camnet a news article by the Inter Press Service (IPS) with details of the arrest and torture of two elected officials of the opposition SDF party. According to the news story, the men were held on suspicion of involvement in "alleged 'terrorist' activities" and allegedly tortured, but were subsequently released without charge.

To some Camnetters, the very act of publishing a news story detailing human rights abuses was perceived as an attempt to tarnish the Biya régime's image. Obviously, I did not subscribe to this view and could not pass up an opportunity to set the record straight.

On September 20, 1998, Kate Atabong wrote:

Hello Mola,

This magnanimity is all the more striking when one considers that Mr. Njawé had already served the majority of his sentence and had only three months left to spend in prison.

Other leaders suspected of having suffered a heart attack would probably have produced a medical certificate to show that despite appearances they were actually in good health. But not our dear Po Mbia, who really "respects our country's institutions." History will no doubt record this aspect of Cameroonian "advanced democracy" as well as the fact that we have "a magnanimous statesman who listens to his people's aspirations and respects our country's institutions."

Long live Po Mbia!

Please correct me if I am wrong but I believe that the two opposition personalities mentioned in this mail have been released from custody without charge. If I can remember rightly, the news of their release was made known to us last week.

Denting Biya's records on Democracy with this one will be a little unfair as these guys have been released without charge and have probably returned home to continue with bizniz as usual.

Peace!!

Kate Fole Atabong.

Date: Sun, 20 Sep 1998 13:04:23 -0400
Sender: CAMNET
From: Isaac Endeley
Subject: **Re: Cameroon News!**

Hi, Kate:

Thanks for your comments. I think you are absolutely right in pointing out that both personalities mentioned in the Inter Press Service (IPS) news story have now been released. I believe it was *Isaha'a Boh* who brought us that news update last week. I'm not sure how IPS works, but I have noticed that there is often a significant discrepancy between the date a story is written and the date on which it is published. In this specific instance, the story appears to have been researched and written whilst the events were still unfolding. Unfortunately, the circumstances had changed by the publication date.

The time lag notwithstanding, what is of relevance here is the way opposition politicians are treated in Cameroon. I don't think it is fair for you to impute motives to IPS by insinuating that the organisation is intent on "denting Biya's records on Democracy with this one". IPS was merely reporting a set of facts. It is a fact that both men are elected officials of the opposition SDF. It is a fact that they were arrested and detained by the government's security forces without charge. It is also a fact that they were being held not in their home towns (Kumba and Douala, respectively), but "at the infamous national gendarmerie headquarters in Yaoundé". In addition, it is a fact that they were arrested on a flimsy suspicion of involvement in "alleged 'terrorist' activities". That they were subsequently "released without charge and have probably returned home to continue with bizniz as usual", as you put it, is hardly a mitigating factor.

If Mr. Biya is concerned about his 'record on democracy' (whatever that may mean in his case), then perhaps he should work with other interested parties to ensure the elimination of arbitrary rule and respect for due process. His record is already badly dented anyway --probably irretrievably so-- and a simple factual report by IPS could hardly make it any worse.

Ciao.

Mola Njoh Endeley.

****

Re: Cameroon-press: Credibility crisis

Introduction

The *Isaha'a Boh* news service, a venture involving veteran Cameroonian journalist Herbert Boh, was for a long time quite instrumental in keeping Camnetters informed through the filing of regular news reports from Cameroon. The reports were generally well researched and fact-based but on occasion the quality of the work left a bit to be desired.

One of the news stories in which *Isaha'a Boh* appears to be expressing regret at the credibility crisis facing Cameroon's independent press triggered another lively debate on Camnet. I personally took the view that "charity begins at home" and that the news agency should first attempt to fix its own shortcomings before criticising others. I pointed in particular to a catalogue of weaknesses that I thought needed to be addressed before the agency could turn its attention to others.

Isaha'a Boh had established a significant following on Camnet by this time and a number of the contributors thought I was probably being too harsh in my assessment of the agency's performance.

On July 19, 1998, P. F. wrote:

YAOUNDE, July 19 (Isaha'a Boh) - A credibility crisis now looms over the budding Cameroonian independent press following the detention at Kondengui Prison of a news source, arrested after the publisher of Le Jeune Detective *Patrick Tchoua, failed to stand by the code of ethics of the profession which calls on every journalist, worthy of the name, to protect his or her source of information, whatever the consequences may be for him or herself. Going from the principle that a journalist will be unable to do his or her job without the help of news sources, the principle of never denouncing news sources is considered as an important requirement for the survival of the profession itself.*

Who, indeed, would provide any information to journalists if that source knew or suspected that it could be delivered to the police for arrest at the first questions thrown at the journalist? Who would have ever spoken to the authors of the Water Scandal had they not been sure the journalists were going to protect them?

Seen from this perspective, there are growing fears that what is now known as the Tchoua-Nana-MINEFI affair, is likely to badly damage the credibility of the Cameroonian press.

Date: Mon, 20 Jul 1998 00:11:45 -0400
Sender: CAMNET
From: Isaac Endeley
Subject: **Re: Cameroon-press: Credibility crisis**

Dear Pierre Faa:

I find it rather ironic that *Isaha'a Boh* should be one of the first to comment on the credibility crisis currently besetting Cameroonian journalism. Any keen observer of Cameroonian affairs knows that all the media outlets have obvious editorial and ideological biases (e.g. pro-government or pro-opposition), and *Isaha'a Boh* is no exception. On my part, I have noticed a number of lamentable shortcomings in many of the stories published on our mailing list and on the web by Mr. Herbert Boh's news organisation over the last nine or ten months. These include glaring factual errors, inaccuracies, inconsistencies and untruthful statements. (Let's leave aside the language quality for the time being.)

Cameroonian journalism is definitely in crisis. But this is nothing new, and revealing a news source is among the least of the problems being faced. Charity begins at home: Mr. Boh should check his own news stories and his own journalistic ethics before criticising other people's.

(Lest I get lynched by his fans, I'd like to point out that I know Herbert Boh personally and that I've taken up these same issues with him privately [via e-mail] on a number of occasions over the last several months.)

Peace to all.

Mola Njoh Endeley.

****

124

Date: Tue, 21 Jul 1998 08:02:32 -0400
Sender: CAMNET
From: Isaac Endeley
Subject: **Re: Cameroon-press: Credibility crisis**

Hello, Aristide:

Thanks for your very instructive and constructive comments. The issues you raise are too important to overlook. However, I hope you will pardon me if I elect to focus my rebuttal on this brief excerpt from your text.

You wrote:

But the larger issue is: how does a serious Cameroonian journalist check the validity of the information he gets from someone in a context like Cameroon where there is lack for accountability and transparency, corruption in the judicial system, over-dominance of the executive branch of the government and where high ranking officials of the administration can do whatever they want when they want?

As an integral part of my response, please find appended below a copy of a recent news story from Isaha'a Boh (first posted on Camnet within the last fortnight by our brother Willie Ade). To my mind the kind of lapses betrayed in this news item are exactly what can cost a journalist his credibility. Unlike you, I don't think any Cameroonian journalist needs a ministerial order or a presidential decree to verify certain basic facts.

You will recall, for instance, that the so-called "terrorist attacks" took place around March 30, 1997, not in March 1996. Anyone who was on Camnet in April and May of last year will surely remember Kamguia Mu Fedjo's valiant efforts to coordinate the petition drive. Such a recollection would naturally cause one to start scratching one's head and questioning the reporter's credibility merely upon viewing the headline. All the more so, given that this erroneous date is repeated in the opening paragraph of the text. As if that were not bad enough, *Isaha'a Boh* goes on to state that the victim (Mr. Akwanga) has been detained "for more than two years already". In the end, one may not treat the story with the seriousness it deserves.

These are the credibility issues to which I was referring. You will surely agree with me, Aristide, that the government has nothing to do with verifying any of these details. I don't particularly enjoy nit-picking, but I hate to settle for anything other than the very best. Not even from my friends and acquaintances.

Best regards,

Mola Njoh Endeley.

****

Cameroon-politics: One of the suspects of March 1996 terrorist attacks in North West wrestles against death

YAOUNDE, July 12 (Isaha'a Boh) - One of the suspects arrested in March 1996 in connection with what the government of Cameroon officially described as "terrorist attacks by secessionist anglophone groupings" in the North West Province Ebenezer Derek Akwanga, is battling for his life at the Mfou Production Prison, some 15 km to the south of the Cameroonian capital, Isaha'a Boh has learnt from reliable sources. Detained for more than two years already and now aged 26, Mr. Akwanga was a student of the University of Buea at the time of his arrest.

After a first period of detention in Bamenda, chief town of the predominantly English-speaking North West Province of Cameroon, Mr. Akwanga was later transferred to the Mfou Production Prison where he is very ill at this moment. News of Mr. Akwanga's deteriorating health was notably confirmed by officials of the Ecumenical Services of Peace (ServiceHumanus) who visited the prisoner a few days ago.

126

"Akwanga does not have access to specialised medical attention which he needs very urgently as he battles for survival", officials of Service Humanus have said.

In a statement, Service Humanus has called on all persons of good will to bring whatever material assistance they can for this prisoner. The statement calls also on specialists (medical doctors and psychiatrists) as well as on lawyers to offer their services to help free Mr. Akwanga.

© *1998 Isaha'a Boh Cameroon*
PO. Box 731 Yaounde, Cameroon, Tel. (237) 20 58 24

****

On July 21, 1998, I.I.B. EBAI wrote:

Mola,

Your recent comments about the credibility crisis facing the Cameroonian press have been poignant and incisive. I agree that the press faces not only a credibility crisis but equally an identity crisis and all sorts of problems. But lest you lend yourself into some credibility crisis as well, can I just point out that you and Mr Boh seem to be referring to two separate incidents? If my memory serves me right and any University of Buea graduate on the net can testify, Mr. Akwanga who was elected student leader was detained some years ago. I don't know details of the circumstances surrounding his detention but I know he was eventually expelled from the university. Alternatively it could just be a case of two Akwanga Ebenezers!!

Regards,
Lilian.

Date: Wed, 22 Jul 1998 02:17:54 -0400
Sender: CAMNET
From: Isaac Endeley
Subject: **Re: Cameroon-press : Credibility crisis**

Dear Lilian:

I'm afraid I don't fully grasp the logic behind your argument. Perhaps you can help me by clarifying your position. Meanwhile, here's how I view the issue:

1) On the one hand, if Mr. Akwanga was already in detention as a result of events that occurred at the University of Buea prior to the March 1997 incident in Bamenda, then there is no reason why Isaha'a Boh should identify him as "one of the suspects arrested ... in connection with [the] terrorist attacks ... in the North West Province".

2) On the other, if he was actually arrested subsequent to those deadly attacks, then the news bulletin should reflect the fact that he has been in detention for a little over a year now (and not "for more than two years already").

You may wish to take another look at the news story before formulating your rejoinder.

Peace.

Mola Njoh Endeley.

****

The Death of Journalist Norbert Zongo

Introduction

In May 1999 I learnt from a posting on Camnet of the death of the celebrated Burkinabé journalist Norbert Zongo. He had been my classmate at the Advanced School of Mass Communication (ASMAC) at the University of Yaoundé in 1983. I was greatly saddened by the news of his death and the suggestion that the régime of Blaise Compaoré may have been implicated in the death. Apparently, Zongo was an outspoken critic of the Compaoré régime that murdered Thomas Sankara. He may have been silenced by those opposed to the free expression of dissent and alternative opinions.

On May 15, 1999, YSANFO wrote:

Le journaliste Norbert ZONGO a payé de sa vie la dénonciation d'une série de crimes commis par le régime de Blaise COMPAORE. Pendant ce temps en France le Burkina Faso est présenté comme étant "un exemple de démocratie en Afrique de l'ouest".
Venez nous rejoindre pour encourager notre juste combat en adhérant à la mailing list burkina-faso@onelist.com et en dénonçant massivement ce crime sur notre forum.[14]

http://www.multimania.com/ysanfo

---

[14] Journalist Norbert ZONGO has paid with his life for denouncing a series of crimes committed by the régime of Blaise COMPAORE. At the same time Burkina Faso is being presented in France as being "an example of democracy in West Africa."

Join and encourage us in our just struggle by signing up to our mailing list "burkina-faso@onelist.com" and by vigorously denouncing this crime on the forum.

Date: Mon, 17 May 1999 17:18:35 +0200
Sender: CAMNET
From: Isaac Endeley
Subject: **Re: Crimes crapuleux au BF**

Cher ami,

C'est avec beaucoup de tristesse et de regret que j'ai appris la nouvelle du décès du journaliste burkinabé, mon frère Norbert Zongo, survenu en décembre 1998. Ce fut mon camarade de classe à l'École supérieure des sciences et techniques de l'information (ESSTI) de l'époque, à l'Université de Yaoundé au Cameroun.

Je viens tout juste de visiter votre site web et je n'en reviens pas ! Après avoir vu et revu sa photo, c'est comme si mon frère Norbert me souriait encore. Un jour ou un autre, les Compaoré de ce monde paieront très cher pour leurs "crimes crapuleux".

Adieu, frère Norbert ! Paix à ton âme et que la terre de nos ancêtres te soit légère.[15]

Isaac Njoh Endeley.

****

---

[15] Dear Friend:

It was with a lot of sadness that I learnt of the death, in December 1998, of the Burkinabé journalist, my brother Norbert Zongo. He was my classmate at the erstwhile Advnced School of Mass Communication (ASMAC) at the University of Yaoundé in Cameroon.

I have just visited your website and I cannot believe my eyes! I looked at the photo many times and it was as if my brother Norbert was still smiling at me. One day or another, the Compaorés of this world will pay a high price for their ignoble crimes.

Farewell, brother Norbert. May your soul rest in peace and may the spirits of our ancestors accept you among them.

On Freedom of Expression on Camnet

Introduction

Not all participants in the Camnet forum had imbibed the spirit of debate by the end of 1997. Some were of the view that their writings and opinions should not be challenged. As such, anyone who dared to criticise their views would be subjected to ridicule and reprimand. I had a different philosophy and took advantage of an opportunity to present it in the e-mail below.

Date: Thu, 27 Nov 1997 22:42:48 -0500
Sender: CAMNET
From: Isaac Endeley
Subject: **Open Letter To Nouk Bassomb**

Dear Nouk Bassomb:

I must take you to task for your rude and vulgar remarks addressed to Cecile Siewe. Like you, I have never met Cecile and have no idea what she looks like. But that should be of no consequence in a virtual community like Camnet. The simple fact that someone challenges your ideas does not give you the right to ridicule their person or to paint a caricature of them. You preach a philosophy of respect for Africans, yet you lead the way by belittling an African person. What is more, this is an African person you admit you have not yet met. If that is what your "Engaged Anthropology" means, then more and more of us will start consigning your messages to the trash can without reading them! After all, it must be a measure of the shallowness of your ideology that the first serious challenge causes you to sink to such pitiful depths. Please endeavour in the future to discuss ideas, not personalities.

Sincerely,
Mola Njoh Endeley.

Chapter VI

On International Affairs

On International Affairs

Introduction

Camnet participants sometimes had the opportunity to conduct discussions on matters such as Cameroon's relations with other countries or even matters totally unrelated to Cameroon. I often found that due to my background as a specialist in international relations, I was in a position to shed some light on key issues. Besides, I enjoyed conducting academic research and I was always willing to share information with others. In this chapter I have attempted to put together some of the material that reflects the general tenor of Camnet debates involving diplomacy, international political economy, and foreign affairs. The first posting below tries to answer a question regarding Cameroon's geo-political position in Africa.

On March 13, 1998, Nicoline Ambe wrote:

Sometimes for social, political or economic reasons, Cameroon is placed in West Africa or Central Africa. Can anyone clarify the dynamics of Cameroon's geographical location in Africa?

Date:	Sun, 15 Mar 1998 15:19:28 -0500
Sender:	CAMNET
From:	Isaac Endeley
Subject:	**Re: Is Cameroon in West or Central Africa?**

Dear Nicoline:

Cameroon is officially in the Central African region. Soon after the creation of the Organisation of African Unity (OAU) in 1963, it was decided that, for diplomatic and caucusing purposes, particularly within the United Nations (UN), the African States should be split up into five regions, namely, Central, East, North, Southern and West Africa. Further, since continental integration (or African unity) has been one of the leitmotifs of the OAU since its inception, it was agreed that this could best be achieved by starting at the regional level. It was on this basis that the regional economic groupings (e.g. UDEAC--now CEMAC--, ECOWAS, SADCC, UMA) were constituted. The primary criterion for the division is geography, meaning contiguity or, in the case of the island nations, proximity. However, other criteria such as cultural ties and trade relations also come into play. Please find appended below a table detailing the *official* geographical distribution (by region) of the 53 African States that are also members of the UN.

It probably needs to be pointed out that it is *mostly* Anglophone Cameroonians who consider their country as belonging in the West African region. This may be due to the fact that during the British colonial era in Cameroon (~1916-1961), the English-speaking parts of the country were jointly administered with Nigeria, which marks the eastern limits of the West African region. Francophone Cameroonians, on their part, tend to have no difficulty placing their country firmly in the Central African region. This, too, has its origin in the fact that during the French colonial administration of Cameroon (~1916-1960), most of the country was considered part of French Equatorial Africa. The latter, together with the former Belgian colonies, today constitute the core of the Central African region. Obviously, the dominant Francophone culture is one of the main reasons why Cameroon today officially belongs in Central Africa rather than in West Africa.

(I would be quite willing to carry out a *private* discussion with you or anyone else who may be interested in exploring the myriad implications of this geographical distribution.)

Best regards,

Mola Njoh Endeley.

****

Geographical Distribution of African States (March 1995)

Central Africa (10 States)

1) Burundi 2) Cameroon   3) Central African Republic
4) Chad   5) Congo-Brazzaville 6)   Congo-Kinshassa (Zaire)
7) Equatorial Guinea 8) Gabon   9) Rwanda
10) Sao Tome and Principe

East Africa (12 States)

1) Comoros   2) Djibouti   3) Eritrea   4) Ethiopia
5) Kenya   6) Madagascar 7) Mauritius   8) Seychelles
9) Somalia 10) Sudan   11) Tanzania 12) Uganda

North Africa (5 States)

1) Algeria   2) Egypt   3) Libya   4) Morocco
5) Tunisia

Southern Africa (10 States)

1) Angola   2) Botswana   3) Lesotho

4) Malawi   5) Mozambique   6) Namibia
7) South Africa   8) Swaziland   9) Zambia
10) Zimbabwe

West Africa (16 States)

1) Benin   2) Burkina Faso 3) Cape Verde   4) Gambia
5) Ghana 6) Guinea   7) Guinea-Bissau   8) Ivory Coast
9) Liberia 10) Mali 11) Mauritania 12) Niger
13) Nigeria 14) Senegal   15) Sierra Leone   16) Togo

Source: Permanent Observer Mission of the OAU to the UN
346 East 50th Street
New York, NY 10022 U.S.A.
Telephone: (212) 319-5490
Fax: (212) 319-7135

Contact: Dr. J. Sorie Conteh, Political Adviser

****

Re: Model United Nations

Introduction

An American student seeking information in order to represent Cameroon on the Model United Nations Conference at Harvard University came to Camnet with a series of questions ranging from women's affairs to the enforcement of international law. Evidently, some of the responses I provided proved useful, judging from the student's expression of gratitude later.

Date: Sat, 6 Dec 1997 19:25:59 -0500
Sender: CAMNET
From: Isaac Endeley
Subject: **Re: Seeking information on Cameroon**

On December 4, 1997, C. L. Gregory wrote:

I am not from Cameroon but I will be representing Cameroon at the Harvard Model United Nations conference in February, 1998. My name is Carol and I live on the East coast of the United States. My college's group has chosen to represent Cameroon at this conference. We are to "be Cameroonians" as much as is possible. We are to represent as though we are from Cameroon.

Dear Carol Gregory:

[...]

You asked:

What are the women's issues in Cameroon?

Everything, really. That includes education, economic and political empowerment, breaking down cultural barriers and taboos, health and social welfare, to name but a few.

Are there currently any groups, government or private, that deal with women's issues?

There is a Ministry of Women's and Social Affairs, headed for the last several years by Mrs. Yaou Aissatou. There are also several inter-governmental bodies, such as some specialised agencies of the U.N. (e.g. UNICEF), as well as a multitude of non-governmental organisations (NGOs), that deal mainly with women's issues. In addition, some of Cameroon's universities (e.g. the University of Buea) now have a Department of Women's Studies.

The men in my group seem to believe that Cameroonian women are not valued highly by the men. I am hoping that they are wrong and I would like to know the truth.

I'm afraid the men in your group may not be too far off the mark. Of course, the reality may vary from one part of the country to the next. But the sad truth is that, generally speaking, women are not very highly valued in Cameroonian society. In some areas, for instance, parents tend to send only their sons to school, considering it a waste of their money to educate their daughters. Pervasive cultural practices and popular perceptions also make it hard for women to exercise certain professions, although their engagement in such professions is not proscribed by law.

If you stick around Camnet long enough, you may get a sense of the real situation from various contributors. As a matter of fact, just a couple of days ago Constantin Bell lamented the plight of Cameroonian women, alleging in effect that 90% of them were excluded from the decision-making process. But his claim might have been something of an exaggeration, which prompted a rebuttal from Annette Ayukegba.

Also, do you have an idea how the Cameroonian government feels about enforcing international law on criminals of war?

If feelings can be judged on the basis of actions, then I think the Cameroonian government feels very strongly about enforcing this aspect of international law. Here are some of the reasons why:

1) In the immediate aftermath of the Rwanda genocide in 1994, several of the perpetrators sought refuge in Cameroon. But as of late 1996, most of them had been extradited to Rwanda or to the International Criminal Tribunal in Arusha, Tanzania. (See: Economist Intelligence Unit, Country Report, 1st Quarter 1997.)

2) One of the main Prosecutors on that Tribunal is a Cameroonian, Mr. Ben Muna (a former President of the Cameroon Bar Association.)

3) Cameroon's current Permanent Representative at the U.N., Dr. Paul Bamela Engo, is a leading expert in international law. During a previous and rather extended tenure in the same position, he played a significant role in codifying international law and at the present time he is also serving as a member of the UN's Commission on International Maritime Law.

4) Cameroon chose to take its ongoing border dispute with Nigeria to the International Court of Justice, a principal organ of the UN, rather than settle it by military means. (During the last several years the two countries have clashed repeatedly over the oil-rich Bakassi peninsula on their southern border. The ICJ is expected to issue an advisory decision on the case by June 1998.)

Peace....Carol Gregory

Peace to you too.

Mola Njoh Endeley

Date: Mon, 8 Dec 1997 20:41:56 -0500
Sender: CAMNET
From: "C. L. Gregory"
Subject: *Re: Seeking information on Cameroon*

Elias Bongmba & Isaac Endeley....many thanks to you both for your input at my request.

I am studying at a small college in Charleston, South Carolina, USA. Our group has been accepted to participate in the annual Harvard University Model UN. Over 200 universities will send teams of students. As you have surmised, I am not officially representing Cameroon. We have selected Cameroon as our host nation so that we may participate in this *mock* United Nations process. It is but a learning process so that we might better understand how the UN system works.

I desired input from Cameroonians because I thought it would add more feeling to the information I have found in books, magazines, print, and electronic media. The words you all write have more passion than those that have been in print for years or even months.

I am studying to be a paralegal with the hopes of going to law school in the future. I did not go into detail in my original post because I did not want to bore you all with details of my personal life. I am pursuing a new career as a result of losing a job I held with the federal government for 19 years. I was a toolmaker in the nuclear refueling of submarines. It was quite a shock when I lost my job but I know now that it was for the best. I am a woman, 42 years of age, and enjoying the college education very much.

I must write a position paper, a working paper, and a resolution for the Legal Committee of our UN conference. My issues will be: The Enforcement of International Law Against Criminals of War, and; Model Law for Electronic Data and Commerce. Another issue that I am interested in is women's rights.

My intention is to use as wide a variety of information sources as possible. This includes personal views and opinions of those from Cameroon. I made my original request thinking that your personal opinions and outlooks would add true Cameroonian flavor to my Harvard UN experience. Please do not believe that I

140

have done no research, I am a frequent visitor of the library. I merely wanted to keep an open mind and draw from the experiences of others.

Many thanks to you for your time and input.

Peace.....Carol Gregory

****

Re: Model United Nations

Introduction

A few months later another student, this time from Manila in the Philippines, also posted a request for information in preparation for an upcoming Model United Nations Conference. The questions were different and presented me with the chance to explore other aspects of Cameroon's diplomacy.

Gil Erez wrote:

Bonjour, je ne parle pas bien le français parce que je suis un élève dans mon école, J'étudie le français. Ici est ma lettre pour MUN, elle est en anglais parce qu'elle est longue[16].

Date:	Sun, 19 Apr 1998 18:03:49 -0400
Sender:	CAMNET
From:	Isaac Endeley
Subject:	**Re: Model United Nations**

---

[16] Hello, I do not speak French very well. I am just a student and still studying French. Here is my letter regarding the Model United Nations. I have written it in English because it is lengthy.

141

Dear Gil Erez:

Como sta? Warm Cameroonian greetings to you and yours in the Philippines. Thank you for your interest in Cameroon's international affairs. Your mastery of both of Cameroon's official languages is quite commendable. I wish my grasp of Tagalog and other Filipino languages were half as good.

You wrote:

Good day, I am a student at International School here, in Manila. Our grade is currently undergoing a project we call M.U.N. (it stands for Model United Nations). We will be doing some debates and voting. I have chosen Cameroon as my chosen country, and I have some research topics to do.

I have come to you, mission to the UN, because I am in desperate need for information. I have checked some of the economic web pages about Cameroon and they have yielded very promising results, but that is only economics. Economics is only 1/4 of my task at hand. Still needing work are Politics, Diplomacy (which I hope you will have a good idea on), and Military.

For an *official* response to your inquiry, you may find it useful to contact the following:

Cameroon Permanent Mission to the United Nations
22 East 73rd Street
New York, NY 10021 U.S.A.

Telephone: +1(212) 794-2295
Fax: +1(212) 249-0533

Attention: Dr. Martin Belinga Eboutou, Permanent Representative

Mr. Jean-Marc Mpay, Chargé d'Affaires

142

Meanwhile, here are some *unofficial* answers to your questions.

Our main debate will be about arms control and security. I will need some information on Cameroon's army, and weapons. It would be great if you could also tell me what is your stand on nuclear control, are you for or against?

I believe Cameroon stands firmly against the spread and use of nuclear weapons. In 1994-95, when the Nuclear Non-Proliferation Treaty (NPT) was up for renewal, Cameroon's UN Representative at the time, Mr. Pascal Biloa Tang (currently Ambassador in Paris), was instrumental in drafting an African common position against nuclear weapons. In recent times Cameroon hassupported most General Assembly resolutions condemning nuclear testing. It needs to be pointed out, however, that this has not always been the case. In the early 1960s, when France was still conducting nuclear tests in the Sahara desert, Cameroon, like most French-speaking African countries, had a lukewarm attitude towards the nuclear test ban issue.

Mainly in politics I need to know about the current govt, elections (how, who gets to vote, who gets the right to vote, are they free or full of fraud ...). If you would please answer these I will be very grateful.

In December 1990 multiparty politics were legalised in Cameroon. There are now about 140 political parties in the country. The current government is dominated by the Cameroon People's Democratic Movement (CPDM) of President Paul Biya. Elections are held at three levels: municipal (every 5 years, last held in January 1996), legislative (every 5 years, last held in May 1997) and presidential (every 7 years, last held in October 1997). The CPDM holds a majority of the seats in the National Assembly and in the municipal councils. The main opposition party is the Social Democratic Front (SDF). In theory, any Cameroonian citizen over 20 years of age, residing in the country and duly registered is allowed to vote. Whether or not the elections are "free or full of fraud" depends

143

on one's perspective. On the one hand, the government tends to overestimate the level of freedom. On the other, the opposition tends to underestimate it. Both sides exaggerate. The truth probably lies somewhere in-between.

Secondly, is military. This is one of the main topics we will be discussing at the convention. We will be debating about arms control and arms in the countries. I would like to know the current military force in Cameroon and also how the country stands on whether to ban all nuclear weapons and the use of Anthrax and a lethal biological weapon. I am also asking for any information about the military, (conscription? status of the arms, any civil wars or wars fought in ...)

As stated above, Cameroon is against all nuclear weapons. I believe the same is true for biological and chemical weapons also (but I have no evidence for the latter two). With regard to conventional weapons, however, I think the Cameroonian government is trying to maintain a military force strong enough to counter real and perceived threats, both external and internal. The ongoing border dispute with Nigeria over the oil-rich Bakassi peninsula is a case in point. (Incidentally, that case is currently before the International Court of Justice, a principal organ of the UN.) Also, there was a small-scale but long-lasting civil war in Cameroon from the late 1950s to the early 1970s. It was fought mainly between the French-backed government forces and a radical opposition movement known as the Union des populations du Cameroun (UPC). This case, too, was brought before the UN just prior to (French) Cameroon's independence in 1960. Unfortunately, the country's military capability is also being used today to suppress political dissent.

The Cameroonian military force is split up into five branches: Army, Navy, Air Force, *Gendarmerie* and Presidential Guard. According to the CIA World Factbook, Cameroon's military expenditure in 1990 was estimated at $219 million (less than 2% of GNP). But that figure appears to have declined to $102 million in 1994. There is no conscription in Cameroon. In theory, all able-bodied males (18-49 years of age) entering the civil service are required to perform military service. However, this requirement is not enforced. The CIA estimates that some 3.5 million Cameroonians are currently eligible for military service. You can visit the CIA World Factbook at:

http://www.odci.gov/cia/publications/factbook/index.html

We will also be debating about child labor and child rights. I need to know how Cameroon stands on child rights and if there is a large amount of child labor in Cameroon.

Cameroon is a member of the International Labour Organisation (another UN agency) and a signatory to many international conventions regarding working conditions and children's rights. Nevertheless, the practice throughout the country is quite different from the lofty principles enunciated in those conventions. Since Cameroon is not an industrialised country, child labour is not often perceived as a problem. The truth is that it is. In rural areas children perform hard labour on family farms. In urban areas they work as street vendors and hawkers. The current economic crisis makes this virtually inevitable. Child prostitution is another growing problem. Meanwhile, fewer children are getting a decent education.

Finally comes diplomacy. Currently I have no information on this topic and I am in desperation. I need to know the amount of embassies in Cameroon and also how the ambassadors are living. Diplomacy is not a major topic, but it is still needed.

I do not have any reliable data about all foreign embassies in Cameroon at this time. However, I have some information to share regarding Cameroon's embassies abroad. In June 1997 (almost a year ago) there were 45 of them. As well as its UN Mission whose address is indicated above, Cameroon has diplomatic representation in the following areas:

* AFRICA (14): Algeria, Central African Republic, Congo-Brazzaville, Congo-Kinshassa (former Zaire), Cote d'Ivoire, Egypt, Equatorial Guinea, Ethiopia, Gabon, Liberia, Morocco, Nigeria, Senegal, Tunisia.

* AMERICAS (3): Brazil, Canada, U.S.A.

* ASIA & OCEANIA (10): Australia, China, Hong Kong (?), India, Indonesia, Israel, Japan, Lebanon, Saudi Arabia, South Korea.

* EUROPE (17): Belgium, Denmark, Finland, France, Germany, Greece, Iceland, Ireland, Italy, Netherlands, Norway, Romania, Russia, Spain, Sweden, Switzerland, United Kingdom.

For further information on these, you can visit the Cameroon Renaissance Association (CRA) web site and follow the link to "Embassies" at:

http://www.maths.uq.edu.au/cra/cra.html

With all that long stuff in hand, I would like to say thank you again, for this would mean a great deal to me and my team.

Always Grateful,
Gil Erez

It's been a pleasure. Good luck with the project and remember to keep us informed on your progress. By the way, when is the M.U.N. Conference scheduled to take place? Do not hesitate to ask should you have any further questions. You can always reach us by e-mail at: camnet@vm.cnuce.cnr.it

Salamate. Ossigi. Paalam ![17]

---

[17] Greetings in the Tagalog language of the Philippines.

Sincerely Yours,

Isaac Endeley.

****

Re: The Free market and Africa

Introduction

From time to time, Camnet contributors engaged in discussions on how to attract foreign investment to Africa in general and to Cameroon in particular. In this segment, I attempted to push the proponents of certain views of international political economy to advance concrete proposals on how to achieve their objectives. The main thrust of my argument was that there was no shortage of ideas and theories, yet few of these had been transformed into action.

Date:	Mon, 17 Nov 1997 22:03:32 -0500
Sender:	CAMNET
From:	Isaac Endeley
Subject:	**Re: The Free market and Africa**

Dear John Mbaku:

I've been following this discussion very closely ever since it was initiated and I've learnt a lot from you, Ade Angwafo III, Jovita Nsoh, Steve Andoseh and all the other participants. Thank you all for the lively debate. However, your most recent contribution appears to contain a number of contradictions and I would be grateful if you could clear things up for me.

On November 17, 1997, you wrote, *inter alia*:

(2) American and other investors are interested in only one thing -- profit. Until Africans can show to these investors that there is profit to be made (and that foreign assets would not be confiscated by some group of opportunistic politicians), foreign investors will not come to the continent, . . .

Isn't it the same profit motive that causes the French to maintain a deathly grip on Cameroon and its economy, for instance? What more do we need to do "to show these investors that there is profit to be made"? Successive Cameroonian governments have already demonstrated to foreigners that our "group of opportunistic politicians" will not confiscate their assets. So why aren't they investing massively in Cameroon?

(4) Africa must reform its laws and institutions; provide structures for peaceful coexistence and sustainable development; mobilize domestic resources for development; then it can look to the international community for investment. Africa has a lot of resources; what is needed is the enabling environment to manage these resources effectively for development.

You have written copiously on this forum (and elsewhere) about the need for genuine institutional reform in Cameroon and other African countries, and your point is very well taken. But at the concrete level, how do you propose to implement those suggestions? How do we progress from these ideas on paper to real actions that will have a direct impact on the life of the average Cameroonian? Very recently, you suggested that those wielding the tools of power and influence back in Africa are not likely to pay much attention to academic research. Yet I must admit that some of your ideas are quite sound. So how do you plan to translate them into concrete action? How do we get past the powers that be to implement all these wonderful proposals? It is sometimes not enough merely to tell us WHAT we must do; it is also necessary to show us HOW to do it. Please clarify.

All the best,

Mola Njoh Endeley.

****

On Debt Relief

Introduction

The exchange below was triggered by a newspaper article on the possible consequences of debt relief. Unlike many Africans, I believe the structural adjustment programmes (SAPs) imposed on us by the international financial institutions were necessary for our own good. I argued, in the first place, that the SAPs had actually had the benefit of weakening dictatorships across Africa, increasing governmental accountability, and fostering the spread of democracy. In the second place, I suggested that if the proposed debt relief could also be made conditional on certain types of acceptable behaviour by the beneficiary governments, then a positive outcome could be assured.

Date:	Sun, 17 May 1998 01:16:47 -0400
Sender:	CAMNET
From:	Isaac Endeley
Subject:	**Re: Why debt relief alone may not be enough**

Dear Cecile:

Thanks for forwarding this piece by Trevor Phillips.[18] While I agree with him that we need to look at the long-term consequences

---

[18] The article by Trevor Phillips is not reproduced here. Titled "Debt relief for the Third World is not enough", the article was originally published in *The Independent* by the Financial Times, Ltd. in the United Kingdom.

of debt relief, I do not share his pessimism and cynicism. I don't think accountants and multinational conglomerates are the only ones who stand to gain from the proposed annulment. With proper guidance and effective guarantees, the funds previously used to service our massive foreign debt could now be channeled towards other areas that will benefit the general population (e.g. education and health care). But such guarantees will have to be clearly stipulated in the cancellation agreements in order to ensure enforceability and compliance. Rather like the SAPs a decade or so ago, this new proposal could be used as another tool to bring Africa closer to genuine democracy.

Unlike many other Africans, I actually support the structural adjustment programmes (SAPs) and the attendant "conditionalities" imposed on our countries by the World Bank and the IMF. In a very real sense, I believe the SAPs are largely responsible for the semblance of democracy and liberalisation currently taking root in Africa. Without them, I doubt that the "wind of change" that blew across the continent in the early 1990s would have had any lasting impact. Indeed, without them the wind might never have blown in the first place.

By drying up the cash flow to several dictatorships, these international financial institutions essentially rendered them more vulnerable to internal pressures. The regimes were *obliged* to liberalise their economy, open up the political sector, legalise opposition parties, organise elections, clean up public finances and be more accountable. The more recalcitrant dictatorships (e.g. Paul Biya's and Mobutu's) were simply starved of resources. This further weakened them as they were by now unable to meet the demands of an increasingly restive population. As students' stipends, workers' salaries, and other entitlements went unpaid for months, the ranks of the disenchanted swelled, with consequences that we all know today. In the end, even Mr. Biya had to succumb to the conditionalities.

It is my sincere hope and wish that an even bigger stick will be dangled alongside the present debt-relief carrot.

Ciao,

Isaac.

****

Cecile Siewe wrote:

Your approval of the SAPs (which I also happen to think were a necessary evil) is tantamount to saying that the African leaders are incapable of formulating and implementing social and economic policies without the paternal guidance of the IMF and the WB keeping them on the straight and narrow. These people have no business running nations.

Date: Mon, 18 May 1998 01:16:55 -0400
Sender: CAMNET
From: Isaac Endeley
Subject: **Re: Why debt relief alone may not be enough**

Hello, Cecile:

Your statement above summarises my sentiment quite accurately. The only way some of these so-called leaders know how to run a country is down the drain. After almost forty years of independence, many African countries are today worse off than they were under colonial administration. The reasons for this are, of course, well known to all of us by now: weak institutional structures, poorly designed laws, and a host of other factors that allow the elites to plunder the state with impunity. Why should we take a second chance with these crooks without the proper institutional guarantees? In Zaire, for instance, the old adage that a leopard cannot change its spots into stripes got a whole new meaning as "Field Marshall" Mobutu (with his trademark leopard-skin hat) managed to amass a personal fortune worth at least four billion dollars while his country

151

regressed into the dark ages. In the absence of sufficient momentum to buttress a bottom-up approach to state reform, we just might have to settle for the top-down version being proposed by the Bretton Woods institutions. Until such a time as our leaders can answer directly to the African people, I have no problem having them answer to our nations' creditors.

It could be instructive at this juncture to take a step back and look at the reasons why the structural adjustment programmes (SAPs) were imposed on us in the first place. In the 1980s, the World Bank and the IMF realised that most of the projects for which money had been lent to us in the past had come to naught. The funds had been mismanaged and/or diverted to private bank accounts abroad. Our African countries proved incapable of reimbursing the loans and in some cases they were unable even to pay the interest due on those loans. Yet they were asking for more credit! It therefore made sense for the money lenders to try to ensure that all future loans would be repaid. Since the primary cause of the failure of past projects was the fact that our institutional structures were maladjusted, adjustment programmes were recommended as a remedy. Obviously, some of the initial consequences are quite painful. However, since the SAPs are always tailored to suit the specific circumstances of each individual country, I remain convinced that any state that follows them to the letter will benefit in the long term.

The question also arises as to why the Bank and Fund didn't propose similar measures earlier on, say in the 1970s, when it was already becoming apparent that the African states would not be able to repay the loans. One answer is that many of these were long-term loans (25 or 30 years) that only came to maturity in the 1980s. Another reason is politics. Cold War politics, to be precise. Western money lenders were afraid of losing their African clients to the Soviet bloc. Somalia's Siad Barre was a prime example of an African leader who excelled at the game of playing off one super-power against the other. Then, within the last ten years, the Cold War ended, the Soviet Union disappeared and the West acquired a monopoly. For the rest of us, it's do or die!

152

And even with an inordinate amount of their GDPs being re-directed to service debts, they and their cronies still manage to pilfer significant quantities of money. What happens when the debts are cancelled and most of the GDP stays in the national coffers?

That is the question. I suggest that very stringent conditions be attached to any debt annulment scheme. Carrot and stick, if you know what I mean.

- Ten years ago, developing countries owed $1400 bn
- today the figure is about $2170 bn,
- this is about 94% of the entire economic output of the Third World
- each baby in the developing world is born owing about $482
- every day, Third World countries pay rich ones about $717m to service debts
- this is 11 times as much as they receive in aid.

This is just too depressing! I'll stop here for now and let others express their views.

Thanks again, Cecile.

Isaac.

****

Re: Controversial Speech

Introduction

In 1998, Mrs. Specioza Kazibwe, the Vice-President of Uganda, made a highly controversial speech in which she appeared to be insulting women involved in abusive relationships. She also summarily dismissed all those clamouring for democracy in Africa as well as those involved in the nascent information technologies. Her speech was subjected to a critical analysis on Camnet and in the end it turned out that she was just another poorly informed and opportunistic African leader attempting to use any means available to cling on to power. The second e-mail below examines key excerpts of the speech and subjects them to rigorous analysis.

Date: Tue, 2 Jun 1998 23:50:41 -0400
Sender: CAMNET
From: Isaac Endeley
Subject: **Re: Controversial Speech**

Dear Nicoline:

Excellent points, and very well articulated! Vice-President Specioza Kazibwe appears oblivious to the fact that one of the primary causes of Africa's poverty and backwardness is the structure of the political systems littering the landscape. I found the following line from your piece particularly a propos:

"Democracy IS food. It is the cure for hunger."

To wit, the most affluent societies in today's world are all liberal democracies with free-market economies! That is no mere coincidence.

Perhaps it is easier to dismiss Mrs. Kazibwe's cheap and insensitive rhetoric when one realises that her boss and benefactor is Uganda's current homicidal despot and warlord, Yoweri Museveni. Even so, I too "am ashamed for Specioza".

Warmest regards,

Mola Njoh Endeley.

154

****

On June 4, 1998, Steve Andoseh wrote:

I'll submit that if we subjected the speech to a systematic analysis, it would by no means be clear cut that the lady equated battered wives with prostitutes or discounted democracy in favor of relief per se.

Date: Fri, 5 Jun 1998 00:24:07 -0400
Sender: CAMNET
From: Isaac Endeley
Subject: **Re: Fwd: Controversial Speech**

Hello, Steve:

I'm quite eager to take you up on this challenge because at this juncture I believe it's the quickest way of resolving this "controversy over the controversy". Allow me to fire the first salvo by quoting straight from the horse's mouth (i.e. from Mrs. Kazibwe's speech). Here's what she had to say about women in abusive relationships:

We talk about prostitution. One time someone wanted me to comment about prostitution in Uganda.

I said: "What you see on the streets is less than 0.1% of prostitutes. Because the moment you get married, you stay in that home, beaten night and day, because of economic security, you are also selling yourself; you are a prostitute." (Clapping).

In other words, any woman who has ever been abused by her man but didn't immediately leave him is a prostitute! After all, in the Honourable Vice-President's opinion, women get married only "because of economic security". Presumably, an economically secure woman would not be stupid enough to get married to a wife-beater.

155

Forget the men's own culpability. Forget the cultural practices and social taboos prevalent in our African societies. Look only at the bottom line (pun intended)!

And here she goes on the subject of democracy which, by the way, is "new" (read "alien") to her:

Then there is something new now -- democracy. "If you are not democratic, we shall not give you money for this." My God, where is democracy when there is hunger? Where is democracy when women are carried on their men's backs to go and deliver? (Laughter) How do you expect to practice democracy in that situation? We all know where we are going. We aspire for our people to eat well, sleep well, be assured of life to see their grandchildren.

Obviously, Mrs. Kazibwe has never paused long enough to contemplate the full implications of the concept of democracy. Someone needs to inform her that we don't need to always expect others to "give" us money or any form of relief. It is obscene in this day and age for anyone anywhere to die of starvation. Yet this obscenity always seems to hit the same tyrannical and despotic regimes. Coincidence? I think not! With properly researched policies and the right institutions, we too can develop viable political and economic systems that will attract foreign investors while encouraging our entrepreneurs to produce goods and services that can fetch a good price on the international market.

My non-rhetorical questions to her are the following: Where is democracy in Africa at those times when there is no hunger? Where is democracy in Africa at those times when women are not about to give birth? How do our African systems perform when they are not in crisis situations? Is it democracy that prevents our people from eating well, sleeping well, and being assured of life to see their grandchildren?

Finally, dear Steve, I'll leave you with the V-P's thoughts on information technology:

*You know, because when you look at this information technology, the TV's
are showing people jumping up and down, hitting small balls, and then the young
people also go to discos and dance the whole night. They don't work, that they
have a right to recreation. You have no right to recreation when you have not
participated in production. (Clapping).*

Upon re-reading these lines, it occurred to me that some
members of the audience might actually have been laughing *at* the
Vice-President rather than with her. To suggest that proponents of
I.T. (i.e. "geeks" :-)) jump up and down, hitting small balls, without
participating in production, is simply preposterous. Mrs. Kazibwe is
an embarrassment not only to Uganda but to all of Africa!

Eagerly awaiting your rejoinder.

Mola Njoh Endeley.

****

Losing A Leader

Introduction

In Cameroon, rumours about the health and possible death of
President Biya have circulated from time to time without triggering
any real emotion among citizens. The death of King Hussein of
Jordan in 1999 therefore presented an opportunity for Camnetters to
reflect on the mortality of our own leaders. Some criticised me for
wishing for the death of our Head of State, but I think such a
conclusion is unwarranted. As humans, we must all come to terms
with our mortality.

Date: Sun, 7 Feb 1999 17:09:16 -0500
Sender: CAMNET
From: Isaac Endeley
Subject: **Losing A Leader**

Dear friends:

I'm sure many of you have also been following this weekend's news broadcasts and bulletins regarding the passing of Jordan's King Hussein. Personally, I've been struck by the apparently genuine outpouring of grief as expressed not only by Jordanians and other Arabs, but also by Israelis and the peoples of other nations the world over. Even in this day and age when every so-called "public sentiment" can be carefully orchestrated by governments, and when it is fashionable to be skeptical, one cannot help but conclude that the departed monarch was genuinely loved and admired by his subjects, neighbours, peers and allies.

This observation leads me to ask the following question: What would be the immediate reaction of most Cameroonians and the international community if our "leader", President Paul Biya, were to give up the ghost today? Any and all thoughts on this would be highly appreciated.

May the Souls of the Departed Rest in Peace.

Mola Njoh Endeley.

****

Chapter VII

On General Information about Cameroon

On General Information about Cameroon

Introduction

The e-mail messages contained in this section of the book deal with a variety of topics that do not fall neatly into any of the other categories discussed in the previous chapters. These range from topics such as the names of Cameroonian cities to the country's educational system or football. As one who strongly believes in the philosophy of sharing information freely through the Internet and other channels, I endeavoured throughout my participation in the Camnet forum to transmit as much information as possible to others. I enjoyed conducting research and, relative to others, I had easy access to huge volumes of information. That is largely what explains my regular involvement in these exchanges. I am pleased to observe that despite the passage of time, a lot of this fact-based information continues to be relevant.

Date: Tue, 12 May 1998 23:34:27 -0400
Sender: CAMNET
From: Isaac Endeley
Subject: **Re: Name Change**

On May 12, 1998, Elias K. Bongmba wrote:

Can someone help me? When was the name Victoria changed to Limbe, and who was President at the time, Ahidjo or Paul Biya?

159

Hello, Elias:

The name change occurred pursuant to a presidential decree signed by Mr. Ahidjo in 1980 or 1981. (I'm afraid Thierry "Le Bantou" Ngoufan got it wrong.) As soon as I can find the time, I will comb through old magazines (e.g. 'Jeune Afrique', 'West Africa') to dig up the precise date and decree number. Rest assured, however, that it was President Ahmadou Ahidjo and not Paul Biya who ordered the name change.

I recall distinctly that the decree came on the eve of Ahidjo's last state visit to the United Kingdom. "Informed sources" in the Fako area stated at the time that the President had decided to implement the change before, rather than after, the visit in order not to give the impression that Cameroon's relations with the UK had deteriorated in the aftermath.

Incidentally, about two years ago there was a heated debate on this forum regarding that name change (Re: "Victoria or Limbe", Camnet, 1996) with some insightful contributions by Pa Fru Ndeh, Dibussi Tande, Pierre Kamguia, Ambe Njoh, Steve Andoseh, and yours truly, among others. I don't think the date of the change was at issue then, but the exchanges certainly made interesting reading.

I have bet a cup of coffee over this.

As one virtually addicted to instant coffee (of the Muyuka variety), I fully sympathise with you. By the way, which way did you bet?

Best regards,

Mola Njoh Endeley.

****

Date: Wed, 20 May 1998 23:01:14 -0400
Sender: CAMNET
From: Isaac Endeley
Subject: **Re: Name Change**

Dear Elias Bongmba, Thierry Ngoufan and Augustine Kange:

As per my promise last week, I have managed to comb through the archives and to do some background research. You will recall that I stated that President Ahidjo ordered the name change just before embarking on his last state visit to the United Kingdom. Here is what I was able to find in support of that claim:

1) 'West Africa' No. 3377, 26 April 1982, page 1165

Cameroon: Victoria renamed
"After the renaming of Zimbabwe's capital, Cameroon has broken a similar tie."

The port city of Victoria has been renamed Nimbe [*sic*], after a nearby river, by order of a decree signed by President Ahmadou Ahidjo.

The Zimbabwe authorities announced recently that Salisbury had become Harare.

Victoria was given its name in 1858 by the Reverend Alfred Saker, in honour of Britain's Queen Victoria, when he founded a Baptist mission there.

During British colonial rule, Victoria was a major port for both West Cameroon and Nigeria. But after independence and unification with French Cameroon, it lost its role to Douala and now handles just one per cent of the country's trade."

161

2) 'West Africa' No. 3377, 26 April 1982, pages 1117-1118

Cameroonian ties with Britain, by David Ndifang

"Cameroon's President Ahmadou Ahidjo's visit to Britain from April 20-24 was the second visit to the United Kingdom since his country became independent in 1960 and reunified in 1961. The visit highlights the long-standing ties between Cameroon and Great Britain.

The United Republic of Cameroon, which came into being a decade ago next May 20, with 58-year-old Ahmadou Ahidjo as the undisputed President, has built a record of political stability and economic growth rare on the African continent south of the Sahara. His government's non-aligned foreign policy has paid Cameroon great dividends, even if sceptics have often blamed him for Cameroon's continuing ties to one of its former colonial masters, France, which is the country's main trading partner, providing more than 43 per cent of its imports and considerable financial aid. Cameroon may be the amalgamation of what used to be the former French and British Trusteeship territories but since independence, the former has played a much more important role in development than the latter. [. . .] "

3) 'West Africa' No. 3378, 3 May 1982, pages 1181-1182
Cover story: "President Ahidjo in London", by Mark Doyle.

4) 'Africa Report' Vol. 27, No. 4, July-August 1982, page 34

5) 'Jeune Afrique Economie', May 1982.

Although none of these references gives the precise date of the name change, I think it is fair to conclude that it occurred just prior to Ahidjo's departure for London April 20, 1982.

Now, Elias, how about splitting that coffee two ways?

Take care.

Mola Njoh Endeley.

****

The Cameroon Renaissance Association

Introduction

Some members of the Camnet community established a group known as the Cameroon Renaissance Society (CRA) with a mandate to coordinate the collection and dissemination of information about the country and to promote the development of a civic culture, among other things. To that end, the CRA set up a website that was intended to be the central repository, a one-stop shop, for all pertinent information about Cameroon.

During the 1990s there was an exponential growth in the number of institutions of higher learning in Cameroon. Some of the old, State-run "institutes" and "centres" were transformed into full-fledged universities while a few privately owned universities were also set up, at least on paper. From just one university in the entire country throughout the 1970s and 1980s, the figure rose dramatically to eight (six State-owned and two private universities) by 1998. As the reader will see in the following pages, the CRA tried to fulfill one aspect of its mandate by compiling and disseminating data about these institutions of higher learning.

Date: Sun, 19 Apr 1998
Sender: CAMNET
From: Isaac Endeley
Subject: **Cameroon's Universities**

Fellow Camnetters:

Several weeks ago it was announced on this network that we were in the process of collecting data on Cameroon's universities with the intention of posting it on the Cameroon Renaissance Association (CRA) web site. The deadline is fast approaching but there are still huge gaps in the data compiled so far. I would like to take this opportunity to invite folks with any bit of information on any of the universities to kindly share it with the rest of us. The purpose of the web page will simply be to provide a one-stop gateway to which anyone interested in finding out anything about any of Cameroon's universities can turn. If, for instance, you have a relative back at home and you wish to help him or her make the best choices in terms of career or courses; or if you wish to know the cost of tuition and the deadlines so that you can channel the funds home in time, this page would be the only source you need.

Please do not be shy about sharing whatever you have. Any kind of information on any of the universities is useful: number of departments or faculties, administrative structure, courses offered, areas of specialisation, competence of staff, mailing addresses, telephone and fax numbers, duration of semesters or trimesters, libraries and laboratories, computers and other equipment, human relations, tuition and other fees, admission requirements, graduation requirements, duration of programmes, variety and choice offered, affiliations with industry and other research centres, availability of accommodation, general environment, living conditions, costs and standards of living, size of classes, advanced degrees, career prospects, weather conditions and average temperatures, realities, myths and perceptions, extracurricular activities, sports and other facilities, etc, etc. Just send whatever you've got and we'll piece it all together.

Your input is highly appreciated.

Isaac Endeley

****

Date: Wed, 10 Jun 1998 23:59:00 -0400
Sender: CAMNET
From: Isaac Endeley
Subject: **Cameroon's Universities**

Fellow Camnetters:

This is to inform you that a preliminary version of the Cameroon Universities Home Page is now online. Please point your browsers to:

http://www.maths.uq.edu.au/cra/euni.html

And be sure to let us know what you think. The page will be regularly updated as our country's university system continues to expand and as more information becomes available. A French version is also in the works. Feel free to supplement the data either by replying to the present note or by sending a message to the e-mail addresses indicated below. We would also like to thank all those who responded to our request for information, particularly Ambe Njoh who pointed us to the official web site of the Ministry of Higher Education and to Sule Nformi's page on BUST. Hot links to both sites are included in our Universities page.

While you are in the Cameroon Renaissance Association (CRA) neighbourhood, remember that you can find out how our glorious Indomitable Lions and other World Cup teams are doing in France '98 by visiting the Cameroon Football Home Page at:

http://www.maths.uq.edu.au/cra/football.html

For the statistically inclined football fans, the achievements of our national and club teams are available at:

165

http://www.maths.uq.edu.au/cra/footstats.html

You can also get the latest news from Cameroon by consulting *Isaha'a Boh*'s Home Page at:

http://www.maths.uq.edu.au/cra/boh.html

Indeed, you can obtain virtually any kind of information about Cameroon (from the complete lists of our Ministries in Yaounde and Embassies abroad to the names and addresses of our cultural associations and businesses in the diaspora) by following the links at the CRA main page:

http://www.maths.uq.edu.au/cra/cra.html

Thanks in advance for your feedback.

Sincerely,

Roger B. Sidje
Isaac N. Endeley

****

Cameroon's Universities

Introduction

The rather lengthy mail below is an attempt to present a complete picture of the Cameroon education system as it stood in April 1999. This was in response to a question posed by an American from the State of Tennessee. No doubt the data compiled and presented here was partially the fruit of the CRA initiative discussed earlier. As I review these lines in 2012, I realise that there have been quite a few changes in the last decade or so. Nonetheless, the image presented here is the way the educational system appeared to be in April 1999.

On April 9, 1999, Rufus Jones wrote:

Hi,

My name is Gladys Jones. I am a doctoral student in Education Administration and Supervision at Tennessee State University, which is a HBCU (Historically Black Colleges and Universities). I am currently writing a paper on the educational system in Cameroon. Unfortunately, I have not been able to find a lot of print material on this subject. However, as a result of my research, I have recently established an email relationship with Sule who is a Cameroonian living in Nashville. He suggested that I contact each of you. I would appreciate any information that you can share about Cameroon's educational system. I would like to get information on early education (e.g. kindergarten, elementary, and high school - I know that you call high school, college), university, post graduate education, traditional or village education, pidgin, etc. Does Cameroon have a national educational policy? If so, what is it? My paper is due on Tuesday, April 13. I realize that this is a lot to discuss and there is little time, but, I do appreciate your indulgence.

As information, my first knowledge of Cameroon was in 1984 when I graduated from Emory University in Atlanta, GA. That year several countries' track and field teams practiced for the summer Olympics which was held in Los Angeles, CA. Cameroon's team was there. My next acquaintance was in 1994 when I received a fellowship to teach at Cameroon OIC in Buea. I spent almost 1 year. Even though I was sent as a teacher, I feel that I learned much more than my students. I recently learned that Mt. Cameroon has erupted. I am very concerned and I am going to try and call my host family very soon.

One last thing, if you know someone from the Buea area with email, please let me know. I would love to establish correspondence.

Thank you,
Gladys A. Jones

Dear Ms. Gladys Jones:

Thank you for your questions and for your interest in Cameroon. Thanks also to Sule Nformi for the reference. My name is Isaac Njoh Endeley and I am from Buea, Cameroon. I will attempt here to provide you with some information on my native country's educational system, but I would like to caution you that I am writing mainly from memory and the data presented here may not necessarily be up to date.

Now, to your questions: "Does Cameroon have a national educational policy? If so, what is it?" The answer is yes, Cameroon does have an education policy, which is designed, implemented and overseen by the Ministry of National Education. The main objectives of that policy, I believe, include: teaching Cameroonians how to read and write in at least one of the two official languages; fostering our national and traditional values; improving our general knowledge of the world around us; and moulding us into responsible and productive citizens. As you surely know already, there are at least two distinct formal education systems in Cameroon: English and French. The bulk of my exposé will be on the Anglophone system, of which I am a proud product.

Part I: Kindergarten

First of all, to the best of my knowledge, early childhood education is not compulsory in Cameroon. However, parents who can afford to do so generally send their children to kindergarten at about the age of three years. In the Anglophone sector of the country the kindergarten is known as a "nursery school" and in the Francophone sector it is called "*l'école maternelle*". Children attend these schools for about two or three years, until the age of five or six years, when they are deemed ready to start attending elementary or primary school (" *l'école primaire*", in French). I believe the vast majority of these "nursery schools" in Cameroon are privately owned, but there are also a few run by the Government (or the State).

Part II: Primary Education

The duration of primary education is usually seven years (from ages five to 12, approximately). This is the only part of a child's education that is compulsory in Cameroon, and most pupils tend to be a little more than 12 years of age by the time they graduate. The number of primary schools across the country is almost evenly split between Government-owned ones and those run by various religious denominations (e.g. Catholic, Presbyterian, Baptist, etc in the Christian parts, and Koranic ones in the Islamic parts). One significant difference is that there are no tuition fees at the Government schools. At least that was the case when I was growing up. In the Anglophone sector, primary education is split up into seven successive classes and at the end of that period the students must take and pass some general exams in order to graduate. These are the First School Leaving Certificate and the Common Entrance Examination. In addition, there are technical, vocational and professional exams that allow students access to specific career paths.

Part III: Secondary Education

After primary school, there are at least three main further channels students can pursue, depending primarily on their family's financial circumstances, but also on the results obtained at the general exams cited above. These are:

1) Secondary/ Grammar Schools, of which there has been quite a proliferation over the last 25 years. The principal operators in this

sector are the Government, the religious denominations, and a growing number of private entrepreneurs. Here again, tuition at the Government secondary schools (GSS) is either free or costs considerably less than at the other types of school. Selection into the GSS was/is supposed to be based on the results obtained at the Common Entrance Examination. In the English-speaking parts, secondary education at these grammar schools generally takes five years, from ages 12 to 17. Students specialise in the arts and sciences, and at the end of the programme they must take the General Certificate of Education (G.C.E.) exam, at the Ordinary ("O") level. If they pass, they qualify for admission into a high school, involving two more years of study, at the end of which they take the G.C.E. exam at the Advanced ("A") level. Success at this last exam opens doors to universities and other institutions of higher learning. By this time the students are aged about 18 or 19 years, perhaps more.

2) Technical/ Vocational Schools, of which, in my opinion, there are not nearly enough. In this sector the Government and private business people appear to be the main operators. (It is not clear why the religious missions shy away from this area.) As the name suggests, the primary purpose of these schools is to train students in the technical/ technological fields, or to prepare them for specific vocations. The duration of the vocational education is generally four years, after which students must take some professional exams. (Caution: My memory gets fuzzy here.) In the old days they took the City & Guilds exam from London, but that is now being replaced by the *"Certificat d'aptitude professionnelle"* (CAP) exam from Yaoundé. Success at either of these exams gets the student into a technical high school or another specialised institution, with a decent chance of securing employment upon completion.

Incidentally, these two categories described above are generally known in Cameroon as "colleges". When I was growing up, many of the colleges were boarding schools, which meant students left home at a tender age to go and live on campus.

3) Apprenticeships/ Institutes. Students with poor results at the end of their primary education, or ones whose parents cannot afford to send them to college, end up learning a trade locally. For instance, they can sign up at the appropriate place to learn how to become a motor mechanic, a carpenter, a tailor, a bricklayer, etc. There are also some institutes where a person can learn how to become a secretary, a typist, a clerk, a chef, etc. The duration of the training varies from one field to the next.

Part IV: Higher Education

With regard to higher education, Cameroon now has some six public universities under the control of the Ministry of Higher Education. The official web site of the ministry is:

http://uycdc.uninet.cm/

Meanwhile, about a year ago a few of us set up an unofficial web site to provide information to those seeking to learn about Cameroon's universities:

http://www.maths.uq.edu.au/cra/euni.html

Here is an excerpt from that site:

Cameroon's Universities

Cameroon's first university was established in the nation's capital, Yaoundé, on July 26, 1962. For over two decades the University of Yaoundé (UNIYAO) was the country's main centre of higher learning, attracting tens of thousands of students from all over the country and from across the African continent. A bilingual institution, UNIYAO's enrollment easily swelled from 600 students in 1962, to 7,000 in 1970, 18,000 in 1984, and to over 50,000 by 1992.

Obviously, the infrastructure created 30 years earlier could no longer sustain the growing student population and it had become necessary to decentralise the country's university system. Furthermore, as UNIYAO had expanded over the years, a number of satellite centers specialising in different disciplines had been created in the provinces. It was now time to transform them into full-fledged universities.

As of May 1st, 1998, Cameroon has a total of eight universities. Six of them are State-owned while the other two are private institutions. In addition, there are about a dozen professional schools affiliated to the universities.

State Universities

University of Buea

University of Douala

University of Dschang

University of Ngaoundere

University of Yaounde I

University of Yaounde II

Private Universities

Bamenda University of Science and Technology

Catholic University of Central Africa (Yaoundé)

Professional Schools

Advanced School of Translators and Interpreters (ASTI, Buea)

Advanced School of Economics and Commerce (ESSEC, Douala)

Advanced Technical Teachers Training College (ENSET, Douala)

University Institute of Technology (IUT, Douala)

Victor-Fotso University Institute of Technology (IUTVF, Dschang)

Advanced School of Agro-Industrial Sciences (ENSAI, Ngoundéré)

Advanced School of Engineering (ENSP, Yaoundé I)

Advanced Teachers Training College (ENS, Yaoundé I)

University Centre for Health Sciences (CUSS, Yaoundé I)

Advanced School of Mass Communication (ASMAC, Yaoundé II)

Demographic Training and Research Institute (IFORD, Yaoundé II)

International Relations Institute of Cameroon (IRIC, Yaoundé II)

I would be remiss to leave out Sule Nformi's excellent page on the Bamenda University of Science and Technology (BUST), which you can find at:

http://members.aol.com/Sucord/unicam.html#Bamenda

I hope you find all of this information useful. Good luck with your presentation on Tuesday, April 13, and feel free to write again if you need more information. By the way, you can always write to the entire Cameroonian community by sending an e-mail to: camnet@listserv.cnr.it

PS:
Since you were once a teacher at the OIC in Buea, I would be interested in knowing where you think that establishment falls within the classification I have attempted to draw here.

For an update on the Mt. Cameroon eruption, you can go to Yahoo.com on the web and do a search for Cameroon.

Best regards.

Isaac Njoh Endeley

****

On Pidgin English

Introduction

Another American student, this time one conducting research on the prevalence of Pidgin English in Cameroon, posted a number of fairly interesting questions on Camnet in August 1997. First, I pointed him to a few research resources, notably the library at my *alma mater*, the Université de Montréal, where I and other

174

Cameroonians conducted linguistic research in the 1980s and 1990s. Then I discussed my personal views about the use of Pidgin in Cameroon.

Jack Haines wrote:

Bonjour et Hello to all participants on CAMNET.

I am a graduate student at Northern Illinois University in the USA. Although my body was born in the US, I have reason to believe that my soul was born in Africa. I look forward to bringing my soul home to Africa very soon.

As a linguist I can think of no more linguistically rich and interesting place in the world than Cameroon. For a thesis topic I have chosen to investigate the use of Pidgin English in Cameroon (CPE). I have had some success in finding information about CPE but I am interested in learning about the present state of CPE right now, from people who have first hand exposure to it.

If I may be so bold, I would like to solicit any comments or information pertaining to the use of CPE in Cameroon. I would like to generate some discussion about this topic and I hope that this is an appropriate forum to do so. If I have made an egregious error I hope that someone will alert me to it.

Some questions I have are: How prominent or wide-spread is CPE? Do many people use it? Is it used only in the home or is it used in media such as television, radio, and newspapers?

I welcome every sort of comment and suggestion. I speak English and French so replies may be sent in either language. I gladly welcome replies in CPE but it make take me some time to make them out :-).

I thank you for any comments and May Peace Be With You.

Jack Haines

Date: Sun, 24 Aug 1997 20:59:41 -0400
Sender: CAMNET
From: Isaac Endeley
Subject: **Re: Pidgin English (Kamtok?) in Cameroon**
(fwd)

Bonjour, Massa Jack:

Welcome to Camnet and congratulations for picking up this very interesting topic. A lot of work has been done (and is still being done) on the subject of Cameroonian Pidgin English (CPE). But, to the best of my knowledge, much of the corpus of literature currently existing is the fruit of research carried out by Cameroonians. It would therefore be nice to get another view from a non-Cameroonian perspective.

During the 1970s and 1980s, the *Département de Linguistique et Philologie* at the Université de Montréal in Canada trained a good number of Cameroonian Translators, Interpreters and other Linguists, and many of them wrote Master's and Doctoral theses on this or related subjects. They are mostly back at home now, working either at the Presidency, the National Assembly, or the different Government Ministries in Yaoundé. However, the fruit of their research is still being proudly displayed on the university's library shelves. You can access these through the Internet, but you may also need to display a little dexterity, since the system seems just a little complicated. You could also try calling the *Bibliothèque des lettres et sciences humaines* at: 514-343-7430. But be ready to try out your French and sharpen your ears to pick up the Québécois accent! I hope you can negotiate an inter-library loan or something.

I imagine similar studies have been conducted in many US and European universities, as well as in Cameroonian ones. There are some experts in this field currently subscribed to Camnet, and I hope they will be able to help you, too.

Meanwhile, you asked:

176

Some questions I have are: How prominent or wide-spread is CPE? Do many people use it? Is it used only in the home or is it used in media such as television, radio, and newspapers?

I believe Pidgin is very widely used in Cameroon, particularly in the (officially) English-speaking parts of the country -i.e. the North-west and South-west Provinces. It is the major *lingua franca* in these areas, but its use also extends to some of the Francophone areas, especially in the big cities of the Littoral and Western Provinces that border the previous two. In the Northern Provinces, too (Adamawa, North, and Far North), which are next-door to Nigeria, it is also frequently used and this facilitates commerce. One study I stumbled upon contends that Pidgin is indeed the most widely used language in Cameroon (but this remains to be verified). Pidgin is used as the first language in many homes where the husband and wife (father and mother) are from different ethnic groups and therefore do not speak the same native tongue. It is also the main language in the market place and in the streets. My personal belief is that in Anglophone Cameroon, most communication is carried out in Pidgin. It is only the official stuff that tends to be in English -- or in French. (There has been some talk, probably facetious, about making Pidgin the official language of Cameroon. But so far, this remains just talk.)

In the 1960s and 1970s, when I was growing up, there were some newspapers, such as *Cameroon Outlook*, that published columns and whole articles in Pidgin. Many Anglophone Cameroonians over 25 years of age will surely remember Ako Aya, the social commentator and gossip columnist whose biting satire, sometimes written and published in Pidgin (in the above newspaper), helped make a number of people literate! But I'm afraid this is no longer the case. There are still some radio broadcasts in Pidgin, by I think the trend may be on the decline. As for television, I don't think I have ever seen or heard any of its broadcasts in Pidgin. (But then, television was not around in Cameroon when I was growing up and I have had very little experience with CRTV.)

177

One major problem you are likely to encounter is that Pidgin is not standardised. As someone has already pointed out on Camnet, different people from different parts of the country tend to speak Pidgin differently. Quite often, this difference is as a result of a direct translation from their respective mother tongues. On other occasions, this may stem from the natural evolution of the language, so to speak. In recent times, the creeping influence of the French language has made the Pidgin spoken in some parts of the country quite difficult to understand, even to 'native speakers' such as yours truly. Many efforts have been made to compile Pidgin glossaries and vocabularies, but no sooner are they published than they are rendered obsolete or outdated. So quickly does the language evolve!

Now, if I may, let me ask you a question: Do you plan to go to Cameroon during your research? It may not be a bad idea to gain first-hand knowledge on the field.

Let me pause here for now, Massa Jack, but I hope to read from you again soon. Good luck with the research, and do keep us informed on your progress.

Ba-bye,

Isaac Endeley.

****

Re: History of Cameroon

Introduction

In this next exchange, I recommended a history textbook to an American researcher about to embark on a journey of discovery to Cameroon. Since online shopping was already well established in the United States by that time, I also suggested an online search for history books.

Nevin Aspinwall wrote:

Dear Fellow Camnetters, I am an American who is going to Cameroon in the Fall to teach and conduct research on the fishes of the rainforest. I have been puzzled at how much animosity there is toward the government and toward the former colonial powers who governed Cameroon. Not wanting to go there in complete ignorance of the people and the country I would like to find a good book on the history of Cameroon and its people. Preferably, I'd like a book that discusses the people of Cameroon before the Europeans arrived. Anybody have a good book to suggest? Thanks for you help.
Sincerely, Nevin Aspinwall in St. Louis.

Date: Sun, 28 Jun 1998 21:53:29 -0400
Sender: CAMNET
From: Isaac Endeley
Subject: **Re: History of Cameroon**

Dear Nevin Aspinwall:

You may find it useful to visit "the earth's biggest bookstore" at http://www.amazon.com. If you do a general search for Cameroon, you will find several titles related to the country's history. One of the more comprehensive works I've read on the subject is by Martin Njeuma, former head of the History Department at the University of Buea. The complete reference is:

Martin Njeuma
"Introduction to the History of Cameroon"
New York, St. Martin's Press, 1990
ISBN 0312038442, Hard cover, 224 pages, $ 55.00.

I believe there's an entry for it at the Amazon site. The work discusses the issues you raise in your mail.

Bonne chance et bon voyage !

Isaac Endeley

****

On the Indomitable Lions

Introduction

Camnet was frequently the venue for discussions on Cameroon's national football team, the Indomitable Lions. The discussions generally centred on the poor management of the team and the attendant negative results that ensued. Very often the conversation spilled over into politics. Nonetheless, overall support for the Indomitable Lions was then, and remains today, a common denominator among Cameroonians. In that connection, I was moved by the idea that some Camnetters and other Cameroonians residing in Japan got together to purchase a good-luck totem for the Indomitable Lions as they prepared for the 1998 World Cup finals in France.

Message d'Innocent Mboudjeka, daté du 3 juin 1998:

Cela n'arrive pas tous les jours!
La communauté Camerounaise de la région de KANSAI au japon (Nara, Osaka, Kobe, Kyoto, Akashi etc) réunie sous la houlette et au domicile du couple Julius-Karen (Osaka) ont décide de faire une collecte pour l'achat d'un TOTEME de bénédiction à l'équipe nationale du Cameroun. Cette bénédiction a été transmise à l'épouse de notre joueur Patrick Mboma qui a quitté le japon et devra remettre le paquet à nos valeureux joueurs. La cérémonie très grandiose s'est terminée très tard vers 22 pm au domicile de Mr Julius Barthson en présence de nombreux amis japonais. Bravo aux Camerounais de la région et initiateurs de ce geste:

Julius Barthson- Karen Faye
Alain Biem
Raph Niba
Urbain Tchoua
Innocent Mboudjeka
Mme Patrick Mboma
Allez les lions et que notre TOTEME vous guide!
Innocent[19]

Date: Tue, 2 Jun 1998 23:50:57 -0400
Sender: CAMNET
From: Isaac Endeley
Subject: **Re: Lions indomptables : la bénédiction qui vient du Japon!**

Cher frère Innocent,

---

[19] Message from Innocent Mboudjeka dated 3 June 1998:

This does not happen every day!

The Cameroonian community in the KANSAI region in Japan (which includes Nara, Osaka, Kobe, Kyoto, Akashi, etc.), meeting under the leadership and at the home of Julius and Karen (in Osaka), decided to raise funds for the purchase of a good luck TOTEM for the Cameroon national team. The good luck TOTEM was handed to the wife of or player Patrick Mboma, who has now departed from Japan and will deliver the package to our valiant players. The ceremony, which was very grandiose, ended at about 10:00 p.m. at the home of Mr. Julius Barthson and was attended by many of our Japanese friends. Congratulations to the Cameroonians in this region and to those who took the initiative to organise this event:

Julius Barthson & Karen Faye; Alain Biem; Ralph Niba; Urbain Tchoua; Innocent Mboudjeka; Mrs. Patrick Mboma.

Go, Lions, and let our TOTEM be your guide!

Merci de m'avoir apporté un sourire à la fin d'une journée somme toute désagréable. Prière de bien vouloir transmettre mes sincères félicitations à toute la communauté camerounaise au Japon. Vous au moins vous savez ce que c'est que le patriotisme. J'espère que votre totem sera bien en vue lors du mondial et surtout qu'il saura se constituer en une véritable bénédiction pour nos valeureux Lions.

Bravo à vous ! Allez les Lions ![20]

Mola Njoh Endeley.

****

On the Power Distribution

Introduction

Some "official" statistics posted on Camnet in early 1999 suggested that the National Electricity Corporation (SONEL) had only about 150,000 legitimate subscribers. Data from other independent sources, such as the international financial institutions and various UN agencies, tended to corroborate this claim. Nonetheless, the reasonableness of the figure was challenged on Camnet. Some members maintained that since a large number of Cameroonians – possibly the majority – obtained electricity by clandestine means, it was inaccurate to suggest that most Cameroonians were without access to power. In my rebuttal below, I

---

[20] Dear Brother Innocent:

Thank you for giving me a reason to smile at the end of a generally unpleasant day. Please convey my sincere congratulations to the entire Cameroonian community in Japan. At least you guys know the meaning of patriotism. I hope your totem will be displayed quite prominently during the World Cup finals and above all, I hope it will prove to be a real blessing for our valiant Lions.

Congratulations to you! Go, Lions!

argued that even if we were to exaggerate tremendously and posit that many Cameroonians were obtaining electric power illegally, the truth would still be that the majority of Cameroonians did not have access to electricity.

On January 22, 1999, Ndzie Germain-Blaise wrote:

Salut Steve Andoseh!

Que penses-tu alors des nombreux foyers à qui on a coupe le courant pour factures impayées? Ont-ils accès ou bien n'ont-ils pas accès à l'électricité ? Encore des termes qui nous poussent à des discussions ... incompréhensibles. Ceci pour dire que le vrai terme à utiliser est le nombre de foyers au Cameroun qui "ont" l'électricité. Mais comme nous aimons lire les statistiques "internationaux", on prend des mots tels que "avoir accès" qui pour moi ne veulent rien dire dans notre réalité. Voila mon point de vue sur ce thème. C'est à nous à résoudre nos problèmes. On doit donc savoir le nombre de foyers qu'il y a au Cameroun et faire un inventaire de ceux qui ont l'électricité effectivement (pas seulement des branchements).

Meilleures salutations.
ndzie[21]

---

[21] Hi, Steve Andoseh!

What would you then say about the numerous where power has been cut off due to unpaid bills? Do they have access to electricity or do they not? Here, once again, are terms that push us to conduct incomprehensible discussions. By this I mean that it would be better to talk of the number of homes in Cameroon who "have" electricity. However, since we like to read "international" statistics, we opt for terms such as "with access to" which, in my opinion, do not have any meaning in our context. That is what I think on this issue. It is up to us to solve our own problems. We should first know how many homes there are in Cameroon and then determine how many of them effectively have electricity (and not just those with proper subscriptions).

Best regards.

183

Date: Fri, 22 Jan 1999 13:56:42 -0500
Sender: CAMNET
From: Isaac Endeley
Subject: **Re: Allow Fair Debate and Discussion**

Hello, Germain-Blaise:

I believe the claims made by Elias Bongmba and Steve Andoseh to the effect that the majority of Cameroonians do not have access to electricity are accurate and corroborated by the evidence. In the run-up to the privatisation scheme imposed on us by the Bretton Woods institutions, our National Electricity Corporation (SONEL) has had to assess its assets. Recent statistics published by the World Bank, the International Monetary Fund, the United Nations Development Programme and the Economist Intelligence Unit (all of them widely publicised on this forum over the last one year or so), seem to indicate that SONEL has approximately 150,000 subscribers only! Now, assuming that each subscription provides 10 Cameroonians with electric power, that accounts for only 1,500,000 people out of a population of 14,000,000. Even if we were to exaggerate tremendously and to conclude that 2,000,000 people obtain electricity by fraudulent means, that would only account for a total of 3,500,000 users, leaving the vast majority --over 10,000,000 Cameroonians-- without access to electricity!

It seems to me to be a matter of common sense.

Best regards.

Mola Njoh Endeley.

****

www.ingramcontent.com/pod-product-compliance
Lightning Source LLC
Chambersburg PA
CBHW050653280326
41932CB00015B/2888